PLANS *to* PROSPER *You*

PLANS to PROSPER You

Find Your
Purpose Through
Jeremiah 29

GEORGE E. SAYOUR

A Division of WINEPRESS PUBLISHING

Unless otherwise noted, Scripture quotations are from the Holy Bible, New International Version, Copyright © 1973, 1978, 1984 by International Bible Society. Used by permission of Zondervan. All rights reserved.

Scripture quotations noted NRSV are from the New Revised Standard Version Bible, Copyright © 1989 by the division of Christian Education of the National Council of the Churches of Christ in the U.S.A. Used by permission. All rights reserved.

Scripture quotations noted NKJV are from the New King James Version, Copyright © 1979, 1980, 1982 by Thomas Nelson, Inc. Used by permission. All rights reserved.

Scripture quotations noted NCV are from The Holy Bible, New Century Version ®, Copyright © 1987, 1988, 1991 by Word Publishing, a division of Thomas Nelson, Inc. Used by permission.

Scripture quotations noted KJV are from the King James Version.

ISBN 1-4141-0765-X
Library of Congress Catalog Card Number: 2006904729

To Jesus, my Lord and Savior,
because You have plans to prosper me.

TABLE OF CONTENTS

FOREWORD

Jeremiah 29 is a letter written to the Jewish exiles in Babylon assuring them that after seventy years God would fulfill His promise to come to them and graciously bring them back to Jerusalem. God called Israel a stiff-necked people ten times in the Scriptures. Each time He delivered them, they turned from Him to worship idols. This time God delivered them into the hand of Nebuchadnezzar, who brought them to Babylon for seventy years. During the exile He said: "For I know the plans I have for you," declares the Lord, "plans to prosper you and not to harm you, plans to give you hope and a future. Then you will call upon me and come and pray to me, and I will listen to you. You will seek me and find me when you seek me with all your heart. I will be found by you," declares the Lord (*God hears the prayers of a repentant heart.*), "and will bring you back from captivity. I will gather you from all the nations and places where I have banished you," declares the Lord, "and bring you back to the place from which I carried you into exile."

In Jeremiah 29:11-14, God is reassuring us of His love and His desire to forgive us and it speaks of His plans of peace and hope. It is always God's plan to prosper those who love Him. In Deuteronomy 8:18, God says that it's through His power we gain wealth. In 3 John 2, the Holy Spirit says, "I pray that you may prosper in all things and be in health just as your soul prospers" (NKJV). In John 10:10 Jesus tells us that He wants us to enjoy life abundantly.

All throughout the Scriptures it's God's desire that we enjoy good health, hope, and prosperity. The cost is simply that we have faith in Him for our salvation and that we obey His word. That's it.

This book is an illustration of how to take to heart and apply Jeremiah 29 in your own life. Through George Sayour's journey we see the struggles and triumphs that a person experiences while trying to fulfill God's purpose for his life. If you follow the steps George outlines throughout this book you, too, will know the fullness of the prophecy that is Jeremiah 29. You will grow closer to God and you will seek God with all of your heart. Then, and only then, will you be able to experience the prosperity that Jeremiah 29 promises.

Rev. George M. Zaloom

ACKNOWLEDGEMENTS

This book is my life's work and, as such, has been shaped by those that have shown me love throughout the years. As I scan my many memories for the faces of all those that have impacted my life it becomes clear that so many are responsible for shaping the man that I am today. What a daunting task it would be to try to thank everyone who has shared in bringing me to the place where I currently stand. I therefore clearly only make a feeble attempt at expressing the gratitude to those who mean so much to me in the words that follow.

First, I thank God the Father, our Lord and Savior Jesus Christ, and my helper, the Holy Spirit. Without your love and grace I would be lost. Thank you for the promise that is Jeremiah 29. Thank you for giving me the strength to tell my story. Thank you for my life and the people you have put in it.

I thank my gift directly from heaven above, my wife Susan. You are the answer to my prayers and I grow to love you more and more each day. Thank you for accepting me despite my flaws and faults. Thank you for allowing me to be me. Thank you for putting up with me for the last five months while writing this book. I look forward to uncovering with you the plans that God has for us. I love you, baby!

Next, I thank my parents, Richard and Jeanmarie, and my grandparents, George and Violet. Your constant guidance and love have made me who I am today. By instilling in me the faith that you all possess you have given me the greatest gift anyone can give. I am so thankful to God for you, the role that you have played in my life, and for your continual support and affection.

I'd like to thank my best childhood friend and sister, Angela. Growing up with you as my companion couldn't have been better. Through the laughter and the tears we have shared so much. Thank you for always being there for me and for showing me the love that an older brother so much longs for from his younger sibling. You are beautiful!

And finally, I'd like to thank everyone else who has been a part of my life. Thank you, aunts and uncles. Thank you, cousins. Thank you, friends. Thank you, deceased loved ones. I will never forget growing up at your houses, the summer vacations, the weekend trips, and all the fun and sarcasm. Thanks for always being there and for helping me to realize the plans that God has for me.

Love always,

George

INTRODUCTION

"For I know the plans I have for you," declares the Lord, "plans to prosper you and not to harm you" (Jeremiah 29:11 NIV). How many times have we seen that Scripture in the last month? These words adorn almost every kind of item: pens, mugs, plaques, frames, and the cover of this book. This is rapidly becoming the catch phrase of this generation of Christians. What is it about this verse that brings a smile to our faces? That makes us feel warm inside? That tells us it's going to be all right? And why do we feel comfort in it? Wasn't it written thousands of years ago to someone else about something very specific? And what about the surrounding verses?

For each of us, those words spoken by God through Jeremiah to the displaced and captive nation of Israel mean something completely different. My grandfather first gave me those words in the summer of 2003. It was a time in my life when I had made great changes and hearing those words was to me a summary of what had just transpired. Boy was I wrong. The plans were barely yet fulfilled. I would come to find that the Scripture that was read to me was not, as I supposed, an affirmation of what had happened but in fact a prophecy of what was to come.

My father also has experience when it comes to this. He has had his share of successes and hardships. Through every hardship, though, he has come out higher and happier than the time immediately before. He has a plaque with this Scripture hanging in his office at work. He has come to realize that the plans are not merely fulfilled; the plans that God has for you are, in fact, a process. A progression. A journey.

As I reflect on the events of my life, I am amazed at how the pieces of time and the decisions that shaped them fit together in an intricate weave that has led me to the place where I currently stand. All of my interactions, even the minutest details, were carefully planned and perfectly orchestrated to land me in the life that I lead today. The major crossroads have taught me lessons about the temptations of the world while at the same time provided opportunities for me to take an active roll in the plans that God has for me. It astounds me to reflect on my journey of being a successful engineer and manager—from leaving it all to pursue a career in teaching. God took a student and made him into an engineer. He took an engineer and fashioned him into a manager. That manager was then transformed into a teacher. In a perfect completion of the cycle, done in such a way that only God could, He has turned that teacher back into a student.

The purpose of this book is threefold. We will take a deep look inside those words that inspire all who read them in an attempt to understand exactly what God means when He says, "For I know the plans I have for you." I will highlight the journey of my own life as a way to illustrate God's faithfulness to the promise that is Jeremiah 29. Lastly and most importantly, you will be given practical steps and concrete actions that you can take to guarantee that you will fully realize the plans God has for your own life.

Part 1

THE SIGNIFICANCE AND IMPLICATIONS OF JEREMIAH 29

"For I know the plans I have for you," declares the Lord, "plans to prosper you and not to harm you, plans to give you hope and a future. Then you will call upon me and come and pray to me, and I will listen to you. You will seek me and find me when you seek me with all your heart. I will be found by you," declares the Lord, "and will bring you back from captivity. I will gather you from all the nations and places where I have banished you," declares the Lord, "and bring you back to the place from which I carried you into exile"

—Jeremiah 29:11-14

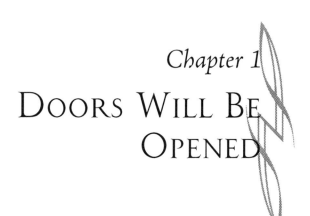

Chapter 1
DOORS WILL BE OPENED

"Ask and it will be given to you; seek and you will find; knock and the door will be opened to you. For everyone who asks receives; he who seeks finds; and to him who knocks, the door will be opened"

—Matthew 7:7, 8

Back in November of 2005 I was purchasing a CD from the local Family Christian Stores. As I was waiting in line to check out, I became lost for a few minutes in the song that was playing throughout the store. It wasn't until the song ended that I realized the customer in front of me (we'll call him Bob) was still occupying the cashier's time. This was supposed to be a quick in and out. What was Bob doing? What is he asking her? He doesn't have any merchandise in his hands, yet he and the cashier seem to be in a serious or even troubling discussion. Bob picked up a pen from the counter and began to jot something down. The next song started to play and I quickly became entranced in it.

As I looked up again from staring off into space, I immediately perceived a noticeable change in Bob's face. It went from a blank confused glare during the discussion with the cashier to an overjoyed and awe-inspired look in just an instant.

Bob's whole demeanor changed just as he had finished writing something down and was handing the pen back. It was just then that he noticed what was written on the side of the pen he was holding: "For I know the plans I have for you," declares the Lord, "plans to prosper you and not to harm you." He looked over at me in amazement and then asked the cashier, "Did you hand me this pen?" The cashier just kind of shrugged. Bob continued, "This is exactly what I've been needing." He handed the pen back and went on his way. There was an obvious change in the demeanor of that believer. I would sum it up by saying that he came into the store noticeably defeated but left obviously victorious.

At that moment I found myself a bit perplexed. We were in a Christian store. Everywhere you turn there were messages of God's hope, love, and grace on just about everything imaginable. There were plaques, frames, mugs, Bible covers, stickers, and yes, even pens with these inspirational messages on them. How could he actually think the pen was meant for him? And besides all of that, doesn't he realize that I'm waiting here to check out and don't really have time for all of this.

I quickly became humbled for I realized the gravity of the words I had been thinking. First of all, how could I claim to be a Christian if the minor inconvenience of waiting a moment too long in a store could set me off like that? Secondly, how is it that I was so wrapped up in myself that I didn't even take a moment to see if I could be of assistance to Bob who was obviously in need of something? And lastly, haven't I myself often seen a Scripture or sign at just the right time and interpreted them as messages from God directly to me?

I really began to think hard about the events that just transpired. Could Jeremiah 29:11 actually mean something to Bob and also mean something to me? Then it hit me like a ton of bricks. It wasn't a matter of Bob and me. Thousands, possibly millions, of Christians use this same verse and it means completely different things to each one. And then I thought one step further. I don't even know the original context of that verse, nor do I know the surrounding verses. Here I am taking to heart and even ownership of a Scripture passage that I know nothing about.

As insignificant as the interaction in the store was, I pondered those events and the questions they provoked inside of me for a long while. I began to reflect on stories of God's faithful servants in times of trouble. In all cases the troubles, obstacles, and trials proved one thing: Locked doors can be opened. I'm not sure what Bob was going through at that time in his life. I don't know what the outcome was or how he is doing now. However, I do know that he left the store that day with a sense of relief and hope. He felt as though a door in his life was about to be opened. I know from my own experience that this is true of the problems in my life and in the lives of those close to me. God has opened doors that were previously locked.

I'm not sure when my first exposure to Jeremiah 29:11 was exactly. My first conscious deliberation about it was when I went into my dad's office and saw those very words framed on his wall.

It was a long and hard journey for my parents. Their original business was located on Miami Beach for the better part of the 80s. But the recession in the early 90s hit them hard and almost forced them to close shop. Somehow or other, though, God had a different plan. He provided the means for them to stay open just long enough to show His faithfulness by opening doors that were previously shut.

In 1992, Hurricane Andrew's Category 5 winds tore through South Florida. I can still remember the events like it was yesterday. Andrew was supposed to strike our neighborhood in North Miami. It was targeted to make landfall around the beach where my parents' business was located. We shuttered up the store and secured the house in preparation to ride the storm out. Well, Andrew ended up hitting about 50 miles away and although we felt hurricane force effects in North Miami it was nothing compared to the devastation that would take place just south of us.

During this time I never really knew how the business was doing. My dad usually kept that to himself. I've since come to find out that it was touch and go all through that time, yet my parents managed to send me to Rensselaer Polytechnic Institute in Upstate New York to study Mechanical Engineering. In my first years of college, things began to go downhill fast for their business. The recession had taken its toll and my father didn't know where to turn since there was no help to be found. It was here that God began to show His grace and my grandfather read these words to my father: "'For I know the plans I have for you,' declares the Lord, 'plans to prosper you and not to harm you, plans to give you hope and a future. Then you will call upon me and come and pray to me, and I will listen to you. You will

seek me and find me when you seek me with all your heart'"
(Jeremiah 29:11-13).

A beautiful thing happened. My father took it to heart and gave his worries up to God. The right people started to cross paths with my parents at just the perfect times. Doors, that were originally closed, miraculously opened. We would soon realize that there was a way to relocate the business and in the most unlikely of places. Hurricane-torn Country Walk from a few years prior was starting to rebuild and thrive. There was a shopping plaza with a space available that fit all of the requirements of the business. The pieces began to fit together perfectly. Even the timing and finances seemed to work out. And through much hard work and the grace of God, the closed doors were opened and the business successfully relocated.

Now to the unbeliever or to someone who wasn't involved in these events this might sound like coincidence or happenstance. I can see how one would think that. But those people obviously don't know my dad. My father is a deliberate and responsible man. He started that business and ran it successfully with my mother for ten years. He is not, however, a man that likes change or complication. In order for my parents' livelihood to relocate it would have to take divine intervention. The timing had to be perfect. If it had happened a minute too soon a suitable location would not have surfaced. If they had waited a minute too late my parents' funds may have been exhausted. Country Walk's rebuilding and availability coincided perfectly with the decline and eventual demise of the original location of their business.

Once my father and mother accepted that this was part of a plan and there was bigger and better on the horizon, opportunities began to present themselves. They offered up their burdens, worries, and fears to the Lord and resigned control of the situation to the One who could take control of it. Locked doors were opened and opportunities abounded.

Control is a funny thing. The hardest times to give up control are often the times when we really don't have it to begin with. It is during the struggles and trials that we most often need to give the steering wheel over to God. Yet we are afraid to let go of the situation and let God guide the way. In Matthew 11, verse 28, Jesus tells His disciples: "Come to me, all you who are weary and burdened, and I will give you rest." Jesus is telling us to turn our troubles, our worries, our burdens, our stresses—all of it—over to Him and He will take care of everything. Yet somehow or other we have trouble doing just that.

Just prior to the time when all of these plans were unfolding, I was trying to figure out where to go to college. I had been accepted to four schools with great engineering programs, one of which was Georgia Tech. Being oblivious to my family's financial situation and the constraints that it would place on us I just figured that I was moving to Georgia in the fall of '93. Well, sometime in the spring (and right around the time when you need to let colleges know your decision), I realized that I couldn't afford to go to Georgia Tech. Georgia Tech is a state college and therefore pretty affordable if you live in Georgia. Being a Florida resident, I would be required to pay out-of-state tuition, which was a considerable amount more. All that was left to do was pray.

Unsure about where to turn, my parents and I just kept an open mind and a praying heart. God would somehow work out the finances and direct me where to go. Up until this point, though, I was dead set on going to Georgia Tech. Just when all hope was lost and we weren't sure what we would do, my parents received a phone call. It was an alumni representative from Rensselaer Polytechnic Institute. An alumni committee wanted to interview me for a local scholarship to the university. Well this was great. RPI was among my top choices along with Georgia Tech. The only obstacle was that RPI's tuition and fees were double that of Georgia Tech's. Could the scholarship potentially make it possible for me to attend?

In the spring of 1993, I sat for the interview with the RPI South Florida Alumni Board. The interview didn't go well at all. The Board focused in on a poor grade that I had received in the first semester of a class that I took senior year. As it turned out, I didn't get that scholarship. I was quite depressed and despair began to set in. Georgia Tech and RPI were my first two college choices. I wouldn't be able to attend either, not because I couldn't get in but because we couldn't afford them. Furthermore, what options did I have left? It was too late to apply to any other schools since the application deadlines had already passed. Everything that I had been working toward for so many years was quickly slipping away.

Of course I began to question why this was all happening. I had been a good kid and followed all the rules. My parents and I prayed and asked for God's guidance. They let me know that God wasn't going to let us down and that He had a plan for me. Then a miracle happened. My mother told me that we would be able to afford RPI. Of course I was confused and didn't know how. She told me that when we were at the interview for the scholarship she and one of the board members had a discussion. Through their conversation he told her to call the Office of Financial Aid at RPI to see if I qualified for any grants, loans, or scholarships that I did not know about. So she did. RPI responded by offering me a financial aid package that included scholarships, grants, a work-study job, and student loans. A door was opened and I could go to college. So I did, and in 1997 I graduated from RPI with a BS in Mechanical Engineering and a Minor in Management.

God knew exactly how to direct me and did so at precisely the right time. His plan was perfectly executed. The scholarship opportunity to RPI had to come up after I realized I couldn't afford Georgia Tech, otherwise I might not have gone. I assumed that I would be going to Georgia Tech, therefore, why would I have entertained the idea of RPI any further? Had I not gone to the interview, my mother would not have known who to place the phone call to and what to ask so I could obtain the grants, aid, and loans that I would need to afford RPI. And of course, had my mother not made that call I would not have gone to RPI.

This chain reaction of events all started with the opening of a door that was previously closed. When all hope was lost, when it was too late to apply to other schools, when I didn't know where to turn, the phone rang. Some people wanted to interview me for a scholarship. The door was opened, the chain reaction began, and events were placed into motion that are still playing out today.

There is another aspect to this whole set of events that is likely the most important. God was not only clearly directing my family; He was, in effect, showing us that He was in control. He let us know that He would make it possible. It wouldn't be through our own efforts but through His grace that this would all work out. Had I done well enough in the interview to get the scholarship, I could have concluded that I obtained the scholarship through my own merits. Had we been able to afford either school, we might have just assumed it was our decision to make. Had our plans worked out without a hitch, we may have left God out of the whole process. The whole situation was an opportunity for God to open and close doors in order for Him to show His faithfulness to us, His servants.

As I reflect on that journey of how God made it possible for me to go to college, I realize that the plans were so much more than that. God wasn't merely providing the means for me to pay for college. He was in effect telling me which college He wanted me to attend. In Isaiah 30:21 we read, "Whether you turn to the right or to the left, your ears will hear a voice behind you, saying, 'This is the way; walk in it.'" Going to RPI for four and a half years was God's will and plan for my life from before I was born. You see, my grandparents were living ten minutes away from RPI as did two sets of aunts and uncles and my cousins. There was also great access to spiritual life on the RPI campus. Some of my greatest memories of my college experience were found at the Chapel & Cultural Center in Troy, NY. God, in His infinite wisdom, knew that I would need this expansive support group to make it through those very trying and rough years of my life. Had I not had the availability and influence of the right friends and family members during those years I'm not sure where I would be today. I can never repay all that my family and friends in New York did and meant to me in those years. God knew that RPI was where I was going and He closed and opened doors to direct me, His servant, into fulfilling His plan.

27

After four and a half years of college I was presented with the next biggest decision of my life. Where should I begin my career? At this time I had been working for the previous two years as a mechanical engineer with a company called Southco. I knew I would have a full-time offer with them once I graduated. General Dynamics had also offered me a job to work on nuclear subs during the summer going into my last semester of college. Over the next four months I would interview with many more companies and landed an offer with Boeing, as well. These were three good viable options. There was one problem, though. None of those companies were where God wanted me to work. This provided God with another opportunity to open doors in an effort to direct me where He wanted me to go.

Out of the blue I received a phone call. It was a representative from Procter & Gamble. They had somehow gotten a copy of my résumé and wanted me to fill out some information for them. I was a little confused because the minimum GPA for P&G was a 3.0. I had a 2.9 and never even thought to submit a résumé to them. Curiosity got the better of me and I decided to go down to the career center and check it out. When I arrived at the center, a P&G representative handed me a thick multi-page questionnaire. The document took about 40 minutes to complete. I wasn't even sure that I wanted to work for a consumer products company but I handed it in anyway. Two days later I received another phone call. I was on my way to catch a flight and was in a total rush. The P&G representative said that they had lost my questionnaire and wanted me to fill out another one. Luckily I had brought a spare one home with me so I completed it and left. They actually sent someone to my place and my roommate gave them the completed document.

I guess they liked what they read because not too long after I was called for an interview. I still wasn't even sure that I wanted to work for them but I went anyway. A couple of days later the phone rang again. I had made it past the questionnaire and the screening interview. The next step was an in-depth interview. I must admit that I was a little turned off by the whole process. I couldn't help but think about all the hoops I was jumping through for a job I didn't even request. Nevertheless, I agreed and went to the on-campus interview waiting area at the appointed day and time. I had arrived a little early and waited patiently. My time came and went and I was never called to the interview room. I decided to inquire at the main desk whether or not the interviewer was behind schedule. It was then I learned that P&G was interviewing in a different building. I ran as fast as I could and arrived for my interview almost a half hour late. I had explained what had happened but was sure I wouldn't get a call back at that point.

Sure enough I received yet another call. This time I had to take a test. "You've gotta be kidding me! Two questionnaires, two interviews, and now a test?!" I'd had it, yet something inside urged me to press on. It was like a challenge now. I went to the room where I was supposed to test and made sure I was early this time. I peered through the glass and no one was there yet. I figured I was just early. Once again, the scheduled time came and I seemed to be in the wrong place. It was then that I noticed a sign on the door stating there was a room change for the test. The test was being held in a building that was a 25-minute walk from where I was. I considered not even going but then I figured I had better. I arrived to take the test 40 minutes late. I'd never filled in bubbles so quickly in my life. An hour and twenty minutes later I handed the test in and once again figured that I wouldn't get the job. The truth was I was really only upset about all the time I had wasted throughout this whole process.

Then out of the blue the phone rang again. Procter & Gamble wanted to give me an interview at their Mehoopany, PA, site. I couldn't believe it. I have heard of people who failed that test. How could I have passed it? I took it as a sign and went to that interview. I was granted an offer soon after.

Now I had a tough decision. In the same way I had wanted to go to Georgia Tech, I really wanted to take the job with Boeing. It would be in Seattle and I was dying to go out West. I was just handed a really tough decision. I prayed and prayed and prayed. I called my parents and asked their advice. God chose to guide me through my mother's tears. She said that she supported any decision that I would make but I knew she wanted me on the East Coast. I chose Procter & Gamble in Pennsylvania.

I know that was a long story but let's take a brief look at all of the mishaps and opened doors throughout that interview process:

1) I never submitted a resume to P&G to be interviewed yet they called me.
2) I only had a 2.9 GPA. P&G required a 3.0 GPA. They overlooked it.
3) My first questionnaire was misplaced. They asked me to fill it out again.
4) I was 20 minutes late for my second interview. They overlooked it.
5) I was 40 minutes late for a two-hour test. I passed it.

This experience taught me one main thing. Nothing can stand in the way of God's plans. I was perfectly content with the job offers I had. God had a different plan. Doors were opened and I went through them. God placed me where He wanted me to be. In later chapters, I will discuss the intertwined events of my life that lead up to, connect, and follow these decisions. Every detail, every event, every circumstance in my life was planned by God. God was not kidding when He spoke the words to Jeremiah: "For I know the plans I have for you," declares the Lord, "plans to prosper you and not to harm you, plans to give you hope and a future. Then you will call upon me and come and pray to me, and I will listen to you. You will seek me and find me when you seek me with all your heart" (Jeremiah 29:11-14 NIV).

Think about those words. Read them again. What evidence is there in your own life that God has a plan for you? What doors in your life were opened when you thought all hope was lost? What decisions have you made that were so obvious at the point when you made them? How did those decisions turn out? What did you learn from them? Read the words again. Do you believe them? Let's look deeper.

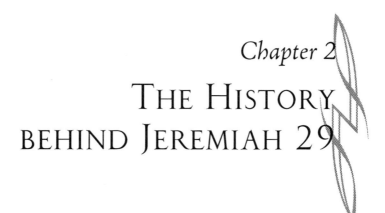

Chapter 2
THE HISTORY
BEHIND JEREMIAH 29

"...I, Daniel, understood by the books the number of years specified by the word of the Lord through Jeremiah the prophet, that He would accomplish seventy years in the desolation of Jerusalem"

—Daniel 9:2 NKJV

Is it any wonder when we read Jeremiah 29 that locked doors miraculously become open, that people find hope in them and are able to see a path through the obstacle course of life, that we feel as if these verses were written especially for us? During this chapter and Chapter Four we will dig into this Scripture that unlocks our potential and gives us hope for what's ahead. But in order to do that, it first becomes necessary to take a look at the author, background, and setting of Jeremiah 29.

Now, it is not my intent to give a history lesson on the roller coaster ride that the nation of Israel has been on from the beginning of time. But a basic understanding of the events that lead up to this prophecy would be beneficial to our understanding of how to appropriately apply this Scripture to our own lives. Read the following passage: "Thus says the Lord of Hosts, the God of Israel, to all who were carried away captive, whom I have caused to be carried away from Jerusalem to Babylon" (Jeremiah 29:4 NKJV).

Did you know that this Scripture is a part of the same chapter of Jeremiah that we are studying? I sure didn't. When I set out to research this topic, I was caught off guard by what I found. The Scripture that begins with, "For I know the plans I have you…" actually was a response to a punishment that God Himself had given the people. Usually when we hear this verse it is in the context of inspiring people to the future, and not about reminding them of their past. But God starts out the letter by saying, "…whom I have caused to be carried away." The curiosity inside urged me to press on.

I was further surprised over this next little tidbit that I turned up. Jeremiah, the prophet through whom God spoke the word, "…plans to prosper you and not to harm you," was actually known as the Weeping Prophet. Well, at this point I didn't know what to think. The very same Bible passage I was using to guide my steps toward happiness was actually inspired by a God who caused the captivity of His people and given to a prophet who was known for his weeping. There just had to be more here that I wasn't getting. A look into the fifth century BC presents a clear case for the basis of these points.

Picture the setting. It is a long time since Israel was captive in Egypt. They had since forgotten the trials and triumphs of their ancestors and the historical relationship between their obedience (or lack thereof) toward God and the results of that obedience. The nation had gone back down the deep and dark abyss of idolatry, immorality, and hypocrisy. It is even noted that they had resorted to child sacrifice during their worship of false gods. To say that destruction was close at hand would be an understatement.

Jeremiah's prophetic ministry began in Judah during this time, between the years of 630 BC and 620 BC. Among the prophets who were his contemporaries or immediately preceded or followed him were Zephaniah, Habakkuk, Obadiah, Ezekiel, and Daniel. Jeremiah's friends were few. The people that he could call acquaintances often turned on him. Many considered Jeremiah to be a traitor because of the messages he sent to the captives in Babylon. He did have a secretary and close confidant by the name of Baruch who recorded the words and relayed the messages that God gave to Jeremiah.

In 605 BC, the Lord lifted His protective hand from His people and Nebuchadnezzar, already on a rampage, besieged Jerusalem. A king was established there and the most skilled and strongest workers were taken to Babylon. Daniel was among the exiled. From 605 to 586 BC, puppet governments that attempted to appease Nebuchadnezzar were placed in Judah. In 586 B.C., Jerusalem was finally captured. Jeremiah foretold of these events in Jeremiah 22:24-30, yet the Jews did not listen.

It's no wonder Jeremiah was weeping. I'd be weeping, too. Of all the times in Jewish history to be born, this had to be the worst since they had lost so much. They had come so far to just forget. Their inheritance of the land and the throne was squandered and all that this generation had to look forward to was captivity and exile. And yet the Jews just didn't understand. Those that were taken to Babylon were looked upon as outcasts, as if they were the ones to have sinned. False prophets spoke of a speedy return home. The Jews all the while were forgetting what was written in their scrolls and spelled out in Leviticus 26:14-46. It was their book, their law, their covenant. They broke it. And so God removed His protective hand from around His people and all of the judgments in Leviticus 26 began to play out.

There are certain rules in science that just can't be broken. If you jump up, you will come back to the earth. If you drive your car into a tree, it will be demolished. It's Newton's Third Law of Motion—for every action, there is an equal and opposite reaction. The funny thing is that it was God's law before Newton was ever born. The Old Testament is packed full of these action–reaction scenarios. In Leviticus 26 we see this more clearly than anywhere else. God is so specific with His choice of words. Verse 3 says, "If you walk in My statutes and keep My commandments, and perform them, then..." And He goes on to list out all the good that will happen over the course of the next ten verses. Then verse 14 says, "But if you do not obey Me, and do not observe all these commandments..." Verses 16 to 39 spell out explicitly what will happen as a consequence to disobedience. Action–Reaction—it should be so simple.

Or is it? About one year ago I really felt like I was walking with the Lord. I was newly married. My wife and I were regularly praying and going to church together. I was co-leading retreats for teenagers. My life was going great. I was heading out on a trip to do some whitewater kayaking in Tennessee. I had planned a stop in Atlanta to visit my aunt and uncle and I was trying to make good time getting out of the state of Florida. Well, I wasn't two hours into the trip when I was pulled over and got a $300 speeding ticket. I couldn't help but feel like God should have gotten me out of that mess. Well, He didn't. Action–Reaction. Even with a full understanding of the laws of the road I still felt like saying: "But God, shouldn't all the good I do preclude me from getting this ticket? I mean, come on, God…"

Right now you're probably thinking that a $300 speeding fine is trivial compared to being exiled from your country. And you're right. But the bottom line is this: Rules exist to protect us and if you break a rule you will face a consequence. It doesn't mean that God will love you any less. Essentially that is what this prophecy is about: God continuing to love His people despite what they did.

This was a time when the people needed to hear from God. There were so many mixed messages that the people didn't know where to turn. In this very uncertain time God, in His love for His people, gave His exiled children very specific instructions. The Lord of Abraham, Isaac, and Jacob gave a message directly to the prophet Jeremiah that Baruch wrote down. This message was delivered by hand to the exiled Jews in Babylon. In the twenty-ninth chapter of Jeremiah, the Jews were told to: "Build houses and settle down; plant gardens and eat what they produce. Marry and have sons and daughters in marriage, so that they too may have sons and daughters. Increase in number there; do not decrease. Also, seek the peace and prosperity of the city to which I have carried you into exile. Pray to the Lord for it, because if it prospers, you too will prosper" (vv. 5-7).

The Jews were very unsettled in Babylon and God knew this. They were, after all, God's chosen people, heirs to the land of their fathers. They couldn't possibly try to get comfortable in another land. They couldn't actually pray for their enemies and captors. Or so they thought. Here God is giving them very explicit instructions to make homes and a life for themselves. They were to pray for this enemy land's success. God wanted them to be settled in their not-so-ideal situation. But He didn't only want them to be settled. Here is the key: He wanted them to prosper. The Lord tells them that as their captors prosper so they shall prosper. You see, we aren't even to verses 10-13 yet. The plan is far from fulfilled. Yet God is telling His people that even in the interim He wants them to be settled and to prosper.

This is so awesome and reassuring! What more can we ask for in a Divine Father? God recognizes that His people are suffering and even though they got themselves into the mess, God gives them the recipe and formula to persevere through it. He tells them via this letter delivered to them His explicit instructions and wishes for how they are to deal with this predicament.

Oh, how I wish I could get such a clear message from God. Too bad I hadn't read these verses earlier in my life. I can't even remember all the times I felt unsettled in school, a job, or where I'd been living. I felt deep down that it was time to move on only to find out it was part of the plan to stay in the situation for a while longer. Isn't it funny how we attempt to justify and gain support for our feelings? We often try to find signs and messages from God to support our own will instead of seeking His will. This is exactly what the Jews in Babylon were doing as we can see in the next verses: "Do not let the prophets and diviners among you deceive you. Do not listen to the dreams you encourage them to have. They are prophesying lies to you in my name. I have not sent them declares the Lord" (Jeremiah 29:8, 9).

It's economics: Incentives Rule. The Jews wanted a swift and speedy return home and the prophets knew this. So they told the Jews exactly what they wanted to hear. "Oh, don't worry. God will restore us back to our land in no time. I feel it. God is speaking to me." Through pressure the Jews got the answer they wanted, but everyone was just fooling him or herself. How often do we do this in our own relationships with people? We may have a friend or family member really struggling with something in life and what do we say? "Don't worry. I'm sure it will all work out in no time at all." We tell them what they want to hear instead of showing genuine support for them. What we should be saying is, "I know that you're hurting. Would you like to pray together about it?"

In the next verse, God addresses this issue of timing. Here the letter changes tone. It goes from giving the Jews instructions on how to deal with the present to a prophecy for their future. Jeremiah 29:10 lets the Jews know that their exile would last for a specified time: "When seventy years are completed for Babylon, I will come to you and fulfill my gracious promise to bring you back to this place" (Jeremiah 29:10). This certainly was not a short time. It would likely outlast everyone who was alive when the exile first took place.

I find it interesting the order in which God chose to reveal His plan to His people. He could have started the letter out with the seventy years prophecy but He didn't. You see, God gave the people His will and instructions before He gave them the bad news. It never ceases to amaze me how God knows the hearts and minds of us humans. The people were looking for a short stay in Babylon. It would have totally crushed them to hear that it would be seventy years and therefore outlast their lives. But God doesn't start like that. He starts by telling them to go about their lives and to pray. He goes on to say that they will prosper even though they are not where they want to live. Once He arms them with actionable items to help them through this tough time, He then lets them in on how long it would be.

And now for the verses of interest: In Chapter 4, we will dig deeper into the specific words of Jeremiah 29:11-13. So here I list them together as the prophecy of hope that the Lord gives His exiled children after He spelled out His wishes for their current situation and the duration for which it would last.

"For I know the plans I have for you," declares the Lord, "plans to prosper you and not to harm you, plans to give you hope and a future. Then you will call upon me and come and pray to me, and I will listen to you. You will seek me and find me when you seek me with all your heart" (Jeremiah 29:11-13 NIV).

We can revel in the splendid way God expressed His plan for His people. We can place those words on signs and plaques and bookmarks and pens. But what do we know specifically of the fulfillment of this prophecy? I know that until I began to write this book I just took it on faith that the prophecy was fulfilled. Admittedly, my knowledge of Jewish history from this time period is not as comprehensive as it could be. However, in light of the fact that I'm writing a book on this subject, I decided to dig a little deeper and to find out the details regarding the fulfillment of the prophecy in Jeremiah 29. I am delighted in what I found and I don't merely mean that the prophecy was fulfilled as we all already assume.

Thank the Lord that even though Jeremiah's message was not what the people wanted to hear (regarding the time frame), there were those who took it to heart. Who, you ask. Well, Daniel for one. In the ninth chapter of the book of Daniel we read,

"...I, Daniel, understood by the books the number of years specified by the word of the Lord through Jeremiah the prophet, that He would accomplish seventy years in the desolation of Jerusalem" (Daniel 9:2 NKJV). This verse was Daniel's acknowledgement of the sovereignty of the Word of God. It said seventy years and it meant seventy years.

What Daniel did next was a direct fulfillment of Jeremiah 29. Daniel prayed. He prayed with all his heart. He knew what the Lord meant in Jeremiah 29:12-13 when He said, "Then you will call upon me and come and pray to me, and I will listen to you. You will seek me and find me when you seek me with all your heart." If ever you are wondering how it is you should pray with all your heart, do yourself a service and read Daniel 9:4-19. In this sixteen-verse prayer, Daniel comes to God humbly, he admits to the sins that brought them this situation, he praises and worships God, and he makes requests on behalf of the people. A whole book could be done on that prayer alone.

Daniel and others of his time knew that they had to pray with all of their hearts in order for the next promise to come true. Verse 14 follows with: "I will be found by you," declares the Lord, "and will bring you back from captivity. I will gather you from all the nations and places where I have banished you," declares the Lord, "and bring you back to the place from which I carried you into exile."

The events that unfold next form one of the most amazing and yet overlooked sets of facts in the entire Bible. Cyrus, a Persian, conquered Babylon in 539 BC. This is a fact that can be confirmed in multiple non-biblical sources, such as the well-respected Jewish historian, Josephus, in *The Antiquities of the Jews*, 10.11.2. Not only was this event foretold, but also Cyrus was called by name. About 150 years before Cyrus was even born and the temple in Jerusalem was destroyed, Isaiah writes in chapters 44 and 45 about both of these events. The Lord says in Isaiah 44:28, "Who says of Cyrus, 'He is My shepherd, and he shall perform all My pleasure,' saying to Jerusalem, 'You shall be built,' and to the temple, 'Your foundation shall be laid.'"

So, what's the point, you ask. Well the point is this: Cyrus was the first instrument by which God chose to fulfill the prophecy in Jeremiah 29. And by making the connection from back in Isaiah (which is also confirmed by the historian Josephus) we can see that this whole set of events was a part of a larger plan. God foretells in Isaiah before Cyrus is born and the temple destroyed that Cyrus would be His *shepherd* and would bring His people back to Jerusalem. Also, in bringing the people back to Jerusalem, the temple would be rebuilt.

Right now you're probably thinking: Well, that's great and all but where is this whole prophecy fulfilled? Well the answer is threefold. God's people were exiled to Babylon in three different phases, approximately nine years apart from each other. In a similar manner, God chose to bring His people back. The exiled Jews returned back to Jerusalem in three different waves.

The first group returned as a result of none other than Cyrus, a non-Jew, who was named in the Bible over 130 years before he was born and had the idea to conquer the throne. For we read: "Now in the first year of Cyrus king of Persia, that the word of the Lord by the mouth of Jeremiah might be fulfilled, the Lord stirred up the spirit of Cyrus the king of Persia, so that he made a proclamation throughout all his kingdom..." (Ezra 1:1). The book of Ezra goes on to describe how Cyrus allowed the Jews to go back and rebuild the temple. And once again this fact is discussed in Josephus's *The Antiquities of the Jews* in 11.1.1.

So there you have it. Let's review. The book of Leviticus summarized the judgments of the Lord due to the disobedience of His people. The Jews didn't heed this warning. God, as part of a larger plan knew this would happen and prophesied through Isaiah that Cyrus would be the instrument by which the Jews would return from captivity and rebuild the temple. Jeremiah foretold of the captivity due to the Jews' refusal to repent. *Then* Jerusalem was captured and the Jews were forced to live in Babylon. During this time the temple was destroyed.

The Lord then prophesies through Jeremiah that He has great plans for His people but they must first wait seventy years to realize these intentions. In the meantime they were to settle down and make lives for themselves. Seventy years had passed and Cyrus, a Persian, took the throne of Babylon by force. He then allowed the first wave of Jews to return to Jerusalem and start rebuilding the temple. This action fulfills both the prophecies in Isaiah and Jeremiah. The further release of the Jews can be found in detail in the books of Ezra and Nehemiah. All these facts are verifiable in extra-biblical works such as *The Antiquities of the Jews* by Josephus.

Through this verse-by-verse historical look at Jeremiah 29:4-14 we, in essence, created a time line that spanned the time from the book of Leviticus all the way to the prophet Nehemiah. Along the way we connected the prophets Isaiah and Daniel as well as the historian Josephus. I'll bet that you didn't know that the words, "For I know the plans I have for you," had such wide-reaching biblical significance. Well, now you do.

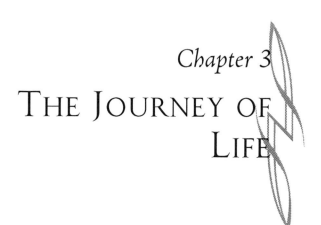

Chapter 3
THE JOURNEY OF LIFE

"Enter through the narrow gate. For wide is the gate and broad is the road that leads to destruction, and many enter through it. But small is the gate and narrow the road that leads to life, and only a few find it"

—Matthew 7:13, 14

Make no mistake about it, God has plans for us. His plans are unique for each of His children. Sure, we all share the same purpose. Our lives are to bring glory to God. But the way in which we fulfill that purpose is different for each of us. Discovering how to best live out our purpose, now that's the hard part. Often in life we get caught not knowing which way to turn and with no conceivable way to change our circumstances.

In a lot of ways our lives mirror that of the Old Testament Jews. In the same way the Jews were exiled to a foreign land, we become sentenced to live out a life without purpose. Each of us goes through times like this. It is during these times that we need a reminder on how to get back on track. We need some incentive to make a change. We need to hear Jeremiah 29.

Each one of us is on this journey called Life. Our parents and society have pretty much laid out for us the direction that we're supposed to go. We start off being good little boys and girls, working hard in school, going to a good college, getting a job, buying a house, getting married, having kids and raising them right, and then we retire. If I had to flow chart this scenario it would look something like this:

Do Good in School → Go to a Good College → Get a Job → Buy a House → Get Married → Have Kids → Retire

Now, I don't know about you but I know that my life took a lot more turns, forks, and bends than that. For some of us, those aren't even destinations on our journey. If you're anything like me, there have been times along the journey when you've felt like you've missed something and your life has been out of balance. It is during these times that we are on one of four paths: The Path of Least Resistance; The Fast Lane; The Scenic Route; or The Road of Regrets, Worry, Depression, and Anxiety. All but the last have some good aspects, but when you operate solely on any of them your life will be out of balance.

THE PATH OF LEAST RESISTANCE

A person who is solely on the Path of Least Resistance has taken the easy way out. When we're on this path we don't want to rock the boat or make waves. Who are we to get in the way of progress? We let things unfold as they will and without consideration. It is during these times that we are laziest and the most complacent. More often than not the Path of Least Resistance leads to discontentment and resentment. These people often feel like the victim but take no steps to correct the situation.

There was a period while I was an engineer that I was so unhappy with work I told myself I would not care anymore. I actually thought that I could pull this off. So I approached work as I thought it should be: just a job. I would just put in my time and leave and not think about it anymore. I operated this way for a few months until I learned that punching a clock didn't fix the inherent reasons for my discontentment. I also learned I'm just not wired this way. It's not in me to not care.

How often are we on this path when it comes to our relationships? When an issue comes up with your significant other or with a parent or child do you address it or pretend that it didn't happen just to keep the peace? You then come to realize that it festered and manifested itself in a big blowout fight or as a health condition, such as an ulcer or high blood pressure. How about at work? Do you do as little as possible so that you are not asked to take on more responsibility? Then do you complain about being passed over?

Paul writes in Colossians 3:23, "Whatever you do, work at it with all your heart, as working for the Lord, not for men." We are not to merely get by or passively allow things to happen. If we are not giving our all, we need to consider what it is we are trying to accomplish. You may have heard the saying: "If something is worth doing, it is worth doing right." I have also heard another version of this same sentiment: "If you're not going to do it right then you shouldn't do it at all." Life on this planet is too short and quite frankly it would be a waste of time to just get by and operate on the Path of Least Resistance.

And most importantly, there is no way possible to fulfill God's plans for us if we are on this path. In Chapter 2 of our study of Jeremiah 29, we see God's instructions for living life on this road. The Jews wanted to just hang out in Babylon until God brought them back to Jerusalem. What were the words God spoke to them regarding this? God said, "Build houses and settle down; plant gardens and eat what they produce. Marry and have sons and daughters in marriage...Pray to the Lord for it, because if it prospers you too will prosper" (Jeremiah 29:5-7). Here God makes it clear that we are to work for and towards our prosperity. We are not to live on the Path of Least Resistance and just let things happen around us. We are to make them happen around us through hard work and prayer.

THE FAST LANE

When you live life in the Fast Lane you are so busy you don't take time to smell the roses. You're completely wrapped up in the activity that you don't have a moment to reflect on the goal at hand. The focus in the Fast Lane is the activity not the results of the activity. When a person in the Fast Lane does reflect on an event they often have regrets about not spending enough time with others, not getting to do what they wanted, or missing out on something.

Early in my career as an engineer I was traveling quite frequently for both business and pleasure. After only a few short years I had amassed about 100,000 frequent flier miles with three different airlines. I would be planning one trip before I even went on the next one. While in the British Virgin Islands,

I was thinking about next month's trip to Cancun. While in Cancun, I was looking at next week's trip to Germany. At work I was trying to outdo and outperform all my coworkers. It was a constant game of one-upping. I made sure that I was on all the right tours and presentations. I tracked every little accomplishment on a scorecard ready to be wielded at any chance to be promoted. In the end all I wound up with were regrets and an ulcer to show for it.

Jesus gave us a clear and concise message about living life in the Fast Lane when He was visiting the home of Martha and Mary: "...Mary, who sat at the Lord's feet listening to what he said. But Martha was distracted by all the preparations that had to be made. She came to him and asked, 'Lord, don't you care that my sister has left me to do the work by myself?'" (Luke 10:39-40). Notice the word that Luke chose to use about the work Martha was doing. It says she was distracted by all the preparations that *had* to be made. He didn't say these were things that Martha *wanted* to do. He didn't say that the preparations *should* be made. He said *had* to be made (or at least they were in Martha's mind). Even this being the case, Jesus responded with, "You are worried and upset about many things, but only one thing is needed. Mary has chosen what is better, and it will not be taken away from her" (Luke 10:41, 42). Martha was so busy with the business of having Jesus as a guest that she missed out on being with Jesus.

Too often in our lives we think that things *have* to be done. The question we need to ask is: What is the expense of this getting done? Are we so busy accomplishing that we are missing out on doing God's work? Are we choosing tasks over spending time with others, as Martha did? We need to remember that God has intentions for each of us. And although He may not operate on our timetable, He is aware of its constraints. Therefore, if you can't get it all done, you're probably not supposed to be doing it all in the first place. Why would God give you more to do than you can handle? I'm afraid this is the path that most Americans find themselves on.

THE SCENIC ROUTE

This brings us to the Scenic Route. The person who never leaves the Scenic Route is unfocused. They are not purposefully living their life. These people are easily distracted. Tasks can become ritualistic rather than to serve a purpose. These people get caught up in everything except that which is important. When they look at their lives, they realize they don't have many accomplishments in their past and aren't working toward any goal in the future. These people are searching for direction and purpose.

Once I got over the unhappiness that I was feeling as an engineer at Procter & Gamble, I thought I would leave and go to another company. I actually had an interview scheduled with IBM. I then realized that all I was doing was running away from one company to go to another one. Procter & Gamble was good to its people and it was good to me. I was making a nice salary and had lots of responsibility. So if I wasn't happy at P&G, what made me think that I would be happy at IBM doing the same thing? I had an epiphany! I would leave engineering and try making money doing other things. I figured that I'd bum around for a while and "find myself." I could be a white-water raft guide in the spring and work resort towns in the service industry the rest of the year. I actually entertained these thoughts for a couple of months. But again I realized I was still running from the situation. I didn't have anything that I was working toward.

We need to be striving for a goal: "But one thing I do: Forgetting what is behind and straining toward what is ahead, I press on toward the goal to win the prize for which God has called me heavenward in Christ Jesus" (Philippians 3:13-14). The Apostle Paul is telling us—no, he is actually urging us—to keep working toward the goal. He says to forget what has happened and strive for something more. He is saying to run toward Jesus, not simply to run away from sin. In my life I was running away from my job but I didn't have direction on what I was running toward.

In Jeremiah 29, verse 11, God declares to us that He has plans for us. We need to be in search of those plans. We need to follow the opened doors and shy away from the closed doors. We need to search for God with all of our hearts. It is not OK to live life on the Scenic Route when our Creator has cared enough to design individual plans for each of us.

THE ROAD OF REGRETS, WORRY, DEPRESSION, AND ANXIETY

This is the catchall of the group. People in this category get caught up in regrets of the past. They worry about the future. They are depressed about the present. When a person is on this road he or she is really missing the point. Jesus died for our sins so that we wouldn't have to dwell on the past but that we should look to the future. The hope of God's plans for us on this earth and what awaits us in heaven is reason enough not to worry about the future. If our sins of the past are forgiven and we have eternal life to look forward to in the future, then there is no reason to be depressed about the present.

I realize that I just oversimplified the real grief and pain that people feel while on this road. It is not my intent to make light of their situation. I am merely boiling all of it down to the three segments. For if our pasts are forgiven and we can look forward to eternal life, we therefore have a present full of possibilities. In all of this there is no need for regrets, depression, worry, or anxiety. In the words of our Lord and Savior in Luke 12:22-25: "Therefore I tell you, do not worry about your life, what you will eat; or about your body, what you will wear. Life is more than food, and the body more than clothes. Consider the ravens: They do not sow or reap, they have no storeroom or barn; yet God feeds them. And how much more valuable you are than birds! Who of you by worrying can add a single hour to his life?"

I used to worry about the future. This primarily took place before I graduated from college. Up until that point in my life I had not accomplished much. Most of my time was spent learning and I wasn't sure if I could apply any of what I had learned. I wasn't an engineer for long before I realized that I was capable and I could accomplish whatever I wanted. I quickly built confidence. Even though I was confident that I could succeed it wasn't easy to avoid depression when things weren't going as I had planned. As for regrets in my life, I have very few. Sure, there are things that I am not proud of. Those things certainly helped to shape the person I am today and without them I would have missed some valuable lessons. I am just thankful to God for His forgiveness and patience with my life.

The most valuable thing I have learned from the times in my life I have spent on this path is that we can't possibly achieve all that God has for us if we are stuck on this road. When we have regrets, when we worry, when we are depressed and anxious, we limit our potentials and abilities and become unable to see the possibilities. We need to shake these concerns and worries of the world in order that we may hear the call of God and head in the direction that He tells us.

THE CALL

It is God's ultimate will and purpose for our lives that we not operate solely on any one of these paths. Somehow or other, though, we often find ourselves on one of these roads to destruction with no way off. We feel that we are too far down the road to make a change, expect anything different, or want something more. This is so unfortunate since we have been created for a unique and specific purpose. We *can* expect different and we *should* want more. Why then are so many of us merely getting by? Why are we too busy to enjoy life? Why don't we know where we're headed? How is it that we just accept our circumstances? Sometimes we even attribute them to God, saying, "It's the will of God." And when things go bad and we want to make a change why is it that we don't know where to turn?

In Jeremiah 29:11-14, God lays out His wishes for us. It only takes one read through those words to know that God is not saying He wants us to just get by. He is not saying that it is His will for us to lead mediocre lives. Just imagine God planning creation. He created the heavens and the earth. He invented science and the rules that govern it. But God didn't stop there. On the earth He put mountains and oceans, and flowers and animals. He painted it all with different colors, shades, textures, and contrasts. Then God created human beings in His image and likeness. Now I don't know about you, but I imagine God's image and likeness to be something so magnificent that words cannot even describe it and if we are created in this very image and likeness we can't be destined in any way, shape or form for mediocrity. We were planned for greatness!

Do you believe this? If you don't, you'd better start to consider it. You'll never make progress towards happiness if you don't even believe that you're entitled to it. Not only are you entitled to happiness, it is God's plan for you. If the only thing you get from this book is this point, then I have done my job. I'll say it again: It is God's plan for each of us to be happy, to *rejoice*. I think Paul said it best when he wrote, "Rejoice in the Lord always. Again I will say, rejoice!" (Philippians 4:4 NKJV).

Of course, these paths may not apply to your life. In my own life I've been on all of these paths at one time or another. There have been times, though, where I've felt like I was right where I was supposed to be and doing just what I was supposed to be doing. For each of us, these hills and valleys can occur at different times. If and when we do find ourselves on one of these roads it then becomes our jobs to decide to correct the situation. We will need to change our mind-set from one that allows us to live our lives without meaning, direction, or purpose to one that puts God in the driver's seat so that we can fully realize all He promises us in Jeremiah 29.

If you are in a situation today that is less than ideal; one in which you are living on the Path of Least Resistance, the Scenic Route, the Fast Lane, or on the Road of Regret, Depression, Worry, or Anxiety, I invite you to say the following prayer:

Dear Lord, I am living life on a path that is not helping me to fulfill Your plans for me. I know the promise that You have given me in Jeremiah 29, verse 11, and I believe this promise. I believe You have plans that involve good things for me. I believe You don't want me to live just a mediocre life. I believe You want me to live a life with prosperity. Please help me to make a change. Help my situation to be resolved. Open the doors that You want opened and close the doors that You want closed. And Lord, give me the strength and courage to go through the doors that You will miraculously open. Give me the strength to follow You and to seek You with all my heart. I ask this in Jesus' name. Amen.

Chapter 4
A STUDY OF THE
WORDS OF JEREMIAH
29:11-13

"The unfolding of your words gives light"

—Psalm 119:130

I know that most of you are reading this book to learn how to accurately apply the words in Jeremiah 29 to your lives. You want to know specifically what it is saying and how to relate it to your lives. We will get to that. We have a whole book left to do just that. In the remainder of the book we will cover such topics as prosperity, making a change in your life, loving God with all of your heart, God's plans unfolding, and His signs to you, among other things. Before we can accurately apply these words, though, we first need to know what they are saying. There are various translations of these verses that may appear to say different things upon first glance. It is the goal of this chapter to sift through the specific words and to understand exactly what they are saying. Then we can proceed with the relevance and application to each and every one of our lives.

Since in Chapter 2 we discovered the context in which these verses were written, it is now possible to look deeper into the specific words of Jeremiah 29:11. No study of Jeremiah 29:11 would be complete without also looking at verses 12 and 13. You see, if verse 11 is the promise, verses 12 and 13 are the conditions of that promise.

How sad it is that we generally pass by the small parts of a verse to get to what we perceive as the meatier component. It is very easy to do and I admit I am guilty of this as well. I have heard that some people have spent an entire lifetime contemplating just one verse of Scripture. Yet in my quest and pursuit of noble goals such as reading the whole Bible in a year or finishing a certain book of the Bible in a day, I often breeze right by the small stuff. I am glad to say that this won't be the case as we study Jeremiah 29, verse 11.

When studying any Bible passage I feel that it is important to examine the verses from at least a couple different translations. Since we are taking an in-depth look at Jeremiah 29:11, I list here five different versions for your reading pleasure. Let's begin.

THE PROMISE

"For I know the thoughts that I think toward you," saith the Lord, "thoughts of peace, and not of evil, to give you an expected end."

—Jeremiah 29:11 KJV

"For I know the plans I have for you," declares the Lord, "plans to prosper you and not to harm you, plans to give you hope and a future."

—Jeremiah 29:11 NIV

"For surely I know the plans I have for you," says the Lord, "plans for your welfare and not for harm, to give you a future with hope."

—Jeremiah 29:11 NSRV

"I say this because I know what I am planning for you," says the Lord, "I have good plans for you, not plans to hurt you. I will give you hope and a good future."

—Jeremiah 29:11 NCV

"For I know the thoughts that I think toward you," says the Lord, "thoughts of peace and not of evil, to give you a future and a hope."

—Jeremiah 29:11 NKJV

For the purpose of consistency throughout this chapter, I will use the New International Version as the major headings of each section. I hope that you took the time to read each of those versions slowly and to absorb what they are trying to say. What? You didn't?! Well, OK. I'll give you a moment to go ahead and reread each one. These different versions use words like *plans, prosper, hope,* and *future.* We also find the words or phrases: *declares, welfare, peace, a desired end.* What is the significance of these words and what are they saying to us? Let's take a look.

"FOR I KNOW...

*"**For I know** the plans I have for you," declares the Lord, "plans to prosper you and not to harm you, plans to give you hope and a future."*

In this very small phrase is the power and true meat of the prophecy. The word *for* is used much in the same way that we

59

use the word *because*. As we saw in the previous verses, God had just told the Jews what to do and that it would be seventy years until they would be freed. This was considerably longer than what the false prophets had told them. So after God tells them this He validates His word to them by saying *because* (*for*). He then proceeds to tell them why.

The word *I* is the key. It connects with the word *Lord* found a little bit later in the verse. The word *I* serves to distinguish between God and the false prophets. God is sternly saying, "It is not the false prophets that are saying this; I am saying this!" God's use of the word *I* helps the Scripture to speak with authority and power. I can almost picture a father speaking to a child where the child is trying to put words in his father's mouth. The father replies, "I know what I'm saying." In other words, don't put words in my mouth.

Know is also very significant to this phrase. Think of all the words that God could have used. He didn't say *guess* or *would like*. He says *know*. When God knows something it is a fact. It is definitive. It is eternal. God is saying that there is no doubt in what He is saying because He *knows* it.

...THE PLANS...

"For I know **the plans** I have for you," declares the Lord, "plans to prosper you and not to harm you, plans to give you hope and a future."

The New International Version uses the word *plans*. Other translations, such as the King James and New King James versions, use the word *thoughts*. When I originally heard this Scripture I had heard it used with the word *plans*. I became a little discouraged when I began to read other translations and saw the word *thoughts* used in its place. As an engineer, the word *plans* just feels so much more concrete. Anyone can think something. But planning something, now that takes thought and effort. Further analysis and a discussion with some friends at work cleared this up for me. *Thoughts* are synonymous with *plans* when it comes to God. God would never think of something that is not in His plan. His thoughts are His intentions. His intentions are His plans. To God, thoughts and plans are one and the same and they equate to His wishes. God is saying here that He has specific intentions for what is about to happen.

Scriptural backing for the explanation of the relationship between God's thoughts and plans can be found in Acts 15:18. Here we learn that, "Known to God from eternity are all His works" (NKJV). So you see, God knows His works from the beginning. What God knows are His thoughts. His thoughts, His works, and His plans are all one and the same.

...I HAVE...

"For I know the plans *I have* for you," declares the Lord, "plans to prosper you and not to harm you, plans to give you hope and a future."

The use of the word *I* shows up again for a specific reason. Let there be no mistake, God is saying that the plans (or thoughts) are His. Not only does He know the plans (the first *I*), they are His plans (the second *I*). If this *I* were omitted the people could surmise that God knew the plans they had. Which of course, He did (and does) know the people's intentions. But here He is clearly saying that the plans He is bringing to action are His.

In other versions *have* is replaced with *think*. The plans that God is thinking are the same as the plans He has. Notice that whether *have* or *think* is used, they are both in the present tense. In other words it doesn't say *had* or *thought*. This is so encouraging because it indicates that God's plans don't change. He thought them before and He thinks them now. Even though the Jews had abandoned Him, He would not abandon His plans. God had these *plans* or *thoughts* before and He still *thinks* or *has* them for us today.

...FOR YOU...

"For I know the plans I have ***for you***," declares the Lord, "plans to prosper you and not to harm you, plans to give you hope and a future."

For is also translated as *toward*. Whether a translation uses *toward* or *for*, the point is the same. It is a gift. God has these plans to give to us. This gift is free to those that receive it and obey His words.

Next we find a very key intention in the use of the word *you*. God used the word *you* to make this inclusive of all who would accept His message. Certainly this verse was specific to the captive Jews. The word *you* in that time referred to all who were captive in Babylon. *You* today refers to all of us captive here on earth. For the Bible tells us that we are "a stranger in the earth" (Psalm 119:19).

...DECLARES THE LORD...

"For I know the plans I have for you," ***declares the Lord***, "plans to prosper you and not to harm you, plans to give you hope and a future."

Declares is translated as *says* in the New King James Version of the Bible. *Says* and *declares* both show that this message is directly from God. It is not what some prophet thinks. God is saying this to them. The difference between *says* and *declares* is similar to the difference between *thoughts* and *plans* that we discussed earlier. When God speaks directly to His people, it is a declaration. He doesn't speak for His own satisfaction. He does so for the benefit of those listening and therefore His words are in actuality a declaration.

The use of the word *Lord* is for a very simple reason. It identifies from whom this message comes. We already analyzed the purpose of the use of the word *I* earlier in the verse. The use of the word *Lord* identifies who the *I* is. And one thing was for sure, this message was not from a false god or some crowd-pleasing prophet. It was declared directly by the Lord.

...PLANS TO PROSPER YOU...

"For I know the plans I have for you," declares the Lord, "*plans to prosper you* and not to harm you, plans to give you hope and a future."

Other translations replace "plans to prosper you" with "thoughts of peace" or "plans for your welfare." As we discussed previously we see the words *thoughts* and *plans* used interchangeably. The major difference between the translations is with the use of the word *peace*. The newer translations have replaced "of peace" with the phrases "to prosper you" or "for your welfare." There are some definite differences here that are not so easily reconcilable between the translations. The answers lie in the difference between how *peace* is used now and how it was used in the time when the Old Testament was written.

Today the word *peace* has very specific connotations. It could refer to a country that is peaceful, such as Switzerland. It could also refer to a state of mind.

Sometimes we use it in the context of a person who has died, as in "rest in peace." In the Old Testament, though, *peace* has an entirely different meaning. It is more complete than just one aspect of a person's life, such as their state of mind. Peace to the Old Testament Jews meant that every aspect of their being, including their physical needs, was taken care of. We can even see this from their greeting of *Shalom*, or "peace be with you." When a person is wished *Shalom* they are being wished a complete and fullness of life, which is also known as *peace*.

Since our current mind-set is not one in which *peace* represents a fullness of the human being, including our physical needs, the translators of more modern versions of the Bible have chosen to use *prosper* or *welfare* in place of *peace*. Whether or not you accept the explanation here for the difference between the words, one thing is clear. God has plans for us that include something good. Call it peace. Call it welfare. Call it prosperity. Whatever you call it, it's going to be good and it's going to far exceed your expectations. In the GSRV (George Sayour Revised Version) we use the word *prosper*.

...AND NOT TO HARM YOU...

"For I know the plans I have for you," declares the Lord, "plans to prosper you **and not to harm you**, plans to give you hope and a future."

Similar to the discussion above regarding the usage of the words *peace*, *prosper*, and *welfare*, we see a difference in how this phrase is translated. *Harm* in the New International Version, shows up as *hurt* or *evil* in other versions. I believe this to be much easier to reconcile than the *peace*, *prosper*, and *welfare* discussion. Evil in Old Testament times was the opposite of good. There is good and there is evil. In modern days, society has minimized the relevance of evil in our lives. Things are no longer good or evil. They have become either good or not good. Evil is a term reserved for monsters, vampires, and dictators in this day and age.

The more modern versions have chosen to use a word that all humans can relate to. They use either *hurt* or *harm*. Again, we can all relate to these words. We can be physically hurt. Or emotionally hurt. Someone can use hurtful words. Our actions can be hurtful toward another. However you slice it, hurt and harm are not good. And good is the opposite of evil. Once again if you are not satisfied with the choice of words between *evil*, *hurt*, and *harm*, let's agree on one thing. God is saying here that He does not plan (or think or intend) for bad to happen to us. And that, my friends, is where the rubber meets the road. The GSRV votes for using the word *evil*.

...TO GIVE YOU...

"For I know the plans I have for you," declares the Lord, "plans to prosper you and not to harm you, plans **to give you** hope and a future."

Well, this is another easy one. No matter which translation you use, this phrase is virtually identical. Here it is in a nutshell. All of the thoughts and plans and good things and not bad things that God has for us are a.... Are you ready for this? All of those things are what? They are a gift. They are a reward. And God is giving those things to...you. What did you do to deserve that gift? Well, you came to God with all your heart in the same way that the prophet Daniel came to God when the seventy years were just about finished. The use of the word *give* here is a direct reference to the words in the next phrase.

...HOPE AND A FUTURE."

"For I know the plans I have for you," declares the Lord, "plans to prosper you and not to harm you, plans to give you *hope and a future*."

Well, if you needed more clarity on the previous section as to what specifically God plans on giving, here it is. He is giving the Jews in Babylon and you and me "hope and a future." Again, depending on your preference for a specific version this may differ by saying "a future and a hope" or "a future with hope." The meaning in all of this is obviously identical.

What I find interesting is the difference between the King James and the New King James versions when it comes to this phrase. In general the difference between the KJV and the NKJV is that the NKJV uses more modern nouns to replace words such as *thee* and *thou*. It also changes some of the words and phrases from the KJV that are no longer used. That is the case when it comes to the use of "a future and a hope." The KJV, instead, originally used the words "expected end."

"Expected end" in this case means an "an end having expectation." It is in essence the "desired outcome." The word *end* used in the KJV refers to the word *future* in the NKJV as well as in virtually all modern translations. In attaining the "expected end," the Jews ultimately could count on a "future with a hope." It was, after all, their expectation that they would be freed and they certainly hoped for it to be soon.

THE CONDITION

Now that we have studied word for word the Prophecy of Hope, let us look at the next two verses. For if we ever intend to realize the plans that God has for us, we first must perform the conditions for which those plans will come to fruition. Let us also look at these two verses from many different angles. Here I present for your reading pleasure verses 12 and 13.

"Then shall ye call upon me, and ye shall go and pray unto me, and I will hearken unto you. And ye shall seek me, and find me, when ye shall search for me with all your heart."
—Jeremiah 29:12, 13 KJV

"Then you will call upon me and come and pray to me, and I will listen to you. You will seek me and find me when you seek me with all your heart."
—Jeremiah 29:12, 13 NIV

"Then when you call upon me and come and pray to me, I will hear you. When you search for me, you will find me; if you seek me with all your heart."
—Jeremiah 29:12, 13 NSRV

"Then you will call my name. You will come to me and pray to me and I will listen to you. You will search for me. And when you search for me with all your heart, you will find Me!"
—Jeremiah 29:12, 13 NCV

"Then you will call upon Me and go and pray to Me, and I will listen to you. And you will seek Me and find Me, when you search for Me with all your heart."
—Jeremiah 29:12, 13 NKJV

It is my contention that these verses you just read which immediately follow verse 11 are actually the lead-up to the plans of God coming true in our lives. You see, God tells us His plans in verse 11 but He doesn't say it will come true yet. He says that He has these plans for us, period. Then He follows with this verse: "Then you will call upon me and come and pray to me, and I will listen to you" (Jeremiah 29:12).

In this verse which follows God's plans for us, God is telling us the first thing we need to do in order for the plans to come to fruition. We need to call upon Him. We need to pray to Him. Ironically, in this day and age people would say that this would be enough. That is because so many individuals don't even believe in God anymore, so just the mere belief in God is all that is required of us when coming to God. Well, that just wasn't so in the Old Testament. And quite frankly it is not so in modern days either.

In Old Testament times, most people believed in a god or in gods. It was not uncommon for people to worship a god publicly. That was, after all, what kept getting the Jews in trouble with the one true God: their worship of false gods. So going to a god and praying to a god was a normal thing to do in the Old Testament times. This is seen clearly in 1 Kings 18:24. The land had been under a sustained drought that was affecting the crops and livestock and everyone's lives. Elijah says to the people, "Let's have a little contest to see who the one true God is." Well, actually he says: "Then you call on the name of your gods, and I will call on the name of the Lord; and the god who answers by fire, He is God" (NKJV).

So you see there was no valor or commendability for people in those days to come to their god when they needed something. That was commonplace. But nevertheless in Jeremiah 29, verse 12, God says that when His people pray to Him, He will listen to the prayers. So basically He's saying, "OK, go ahead. I'll hear what you have to say." He is not yet saying, "Oh, good. You prayed. Well here's the prosperity you want." There is one more step and this is the true condition of the reception of God's blessings. This can be found in verse 13. "And you will seek Me and find Me, when you search for Me with all your heart" (Jeremiah 29:13 NKJV).

Ah ha! There it is: The true condition and really the *heart* of the issue. We must seek God and we must do so with all our heart. It is not merely enough to say an "Our Father" and then expect our reward. God wants to connect with us on a spiritual level. He wants to be discovered; He wants to be found. God wants to be an object of desire. I know that sounds a little quirky or even irreverent to some but it's true. All throughout the Bible this condition comes up. Let's read what Deuteronomy 4:29, 30 has to say on the topic: "But from there you will seek the Lord your God, and you will find Him, if you seek Him with all of your heart and with all of your soul. When you are in distress and these things come upon you in the latter days, when you turn to the Lord your God and obey His voice (for the Lord your God is a merciful God), He will not forsake you nor destroy you, nor forget the covenant of your fathers which He swore to them" (NKJV).

In these words that Moses spoke to the people we see clearly that we are to come to the Lord with all our hearts. And if we do this we will find Him. How awesome is that! All of our dreams will come true. All of God's plans for us will begin to happen. In order to enjoy the riches that God has for our lives and the promises of Jeremiah 29:11, all we have to do is come to the Lord our God and do so with our hearts. Isn't it amazing how easy this sounds yet each of us so often fails to do this?

In Chapter 11 we will dig deeper into this issue. We will investigate what exactly it means to love and seek God with all our hearts. As you read the chapters up until that point, I challenge you to ponder what that means. What does it mean to seek and love God with all your heart?

Chapter 5
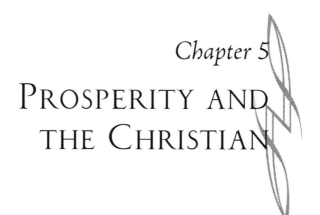

PROSPERITY AND THE CHRISTIAN

"What good will it be for a man if he gains the whole world, yet he forfeits his soul."

—Matthew 16:26

"I have come that they may have life, and have it to the full"
—John 10:10

There is this unspoken assumption among many believers that Christians just aren't supposed to have wealth and prosperity. This is one reason that so many of us become content with the specific path we are on. We feel we are doing what we are supposed to be doing. And we actually feel, deep down in places we don't talk about, that we aren't supposed to have or even want more.

Now of course, we should always be thankful for what we have. Every one of us reading this book today has more than most people in this world. I can say this with certainty because even a poor person in America is not poor by the standards of any of the third world countries around the globe. So, no matter what our particular situation, we all need to give thanks to God for what we have and realize that the true prosperity that we are searching for is the prosperity of the soul. We just need to be open to the fact that the plans God has for us often will include giving us more and leaving us better off than our current state. Since a key part of Jeremiah 29 is prosperity, I thought we'd take a look at what the Bible has to say on the subject.

BIBLICAL EVIDENCE OF PROSPERITY AS A GIFT FROM GOD

The Bible flat-out tells us that we can expect more. The whole point of Jeremiah 29 is to expect more once we've fulfilled the condition. In Deuteronomy 29:9, Moses delivers a message from God to the Israelites and says, "Carefully follow the terms of this covenant, so that you may prosper in everything you do." We see here that if the Israelites obey the covenant, then they can expect to prosper. Now you might be thinking that this is specific to the Israelites at the time of Moses. This issue is addressed as we get to verse 14: "I am making this covenant, with its oath, not only with you who are standing here with us today in the presence of the Lord our God but also with those who are not here today." That's you and me!

That promise applies to all of us who would keep this covenant. The specifics of the covenant can be found throughout the pages of Deuteronomy. Jesus Himself summed this up when He was asked what the greatest commandment was. In Matthew 22:37-39, Jesus replied, "Love the Lord your God with all your heart and with all your soul and with all your mind and with all your strength. The second is this: Love your neighbor as your-self." If you're wondering how we know this refers to the same covenant Moses spoke to the Israelites in Deuteronomy 29, we need to read just one more verse. In verse 40 Jesus says, "All the Law and the Prophets hang on these two commandments."

Prosperity is a gift from God. It is a reward payable upon receipt of the condition to love the Lord with all our hearts as Jeremiah 29:13 tells us. There are a number of other Scriptures that back this claim. Some of them are:

> "Then the Lord your God will restore your fortunes."
> —Deuteronomy 30:2

> "The Lord will grant you abundant prosperity…"
> —Deuteronomy 28:11

> "…but he who trusts in the Lord will prosper."
> —Proverbs 28:25

> "Wealth and honor come from you."
> —1 Chronicles 29:12

> "…when God gives any man wealth and possessions…"
> —Ecclesiastes 5:19

PROSPEROUS INDIVIDUALS IN THE OLD TESTAMENT

It is obvious from those Scriptures that the Old Testament describes a cause and effect relationship between earnestly loving God and the gift of prosperity. Jeremiah 29 clearly speaks to this relationship. But the question that begs to be asked is: When else does it happen? The answer can be seen no more simply and clearly than in I Chronicles 4:10 with the ever-so-brief story of Jabez. Here we read: "Jabez cried out to the God of Israel, 'Oh that you would bless me and enlarge my territory! Let your hand be with me, and keep me from harm so that I will be free from pain.'" And God granted his request. That's all we know about Jabez. What more do we need to know? He came to God earnestly and made a request for prosperity and God granted it.

King David is the next great example of this cause and effect relationship. God had decided that the next king of Israel would be one of Jesse's sons. When Samuel went to Bethlehem to anoint God's choice for the next king, he immediately thought it would be Eliab due to his appearance. In 1 Samuel 16:7, God responds to Samuel's assumption with: "The Lord does not look at the things that man looks at. Man looks at the outward appearance, but the Lord looks at the heart." After rejecting the first seven of Jesse's sons, David was anointed as the next king. Samuel told King Saul how God felt about David when he said, "The Lord has sought out a man after his own heart and appointed him leader of his people" (1 Samuel 13:14). In case there is any question as to King David's prosperity, we read in 1 Chronicles 29:28 that "he died at a good old age, having enjoyed long life, wealth, and honor."

When King David was about to die, he had a little father-son chat with his son and successor, Solomon. Here is what King David said to his heir during that intimate moment: "Walk in His ways, and keep His decrees and commands, His laws and requirements, as written in the Law of Moses, that you may prosper in all you do and wherever you go" (1 Kings 2:3). David then died, Solomon became king, and in 1 Kings 3:3 we see that

"Solomon showed his love for the Lord by walking according to the statutes of his father David."

It wasn't long after Solomon had proved himself to the Lord that God appeared to him in a dream. Solomon was given the opportunity to ask for whatever he wanted. In a prayer to God, King Solomon says: "So give your servant a discerning heart to govern your people and to distinguish between right and wrong" (1 Kings 3:9). He didn't ask for riches or power or prestige. Solomon merely asked for wisdom. God's response to this humble request was to make Solomon the wisest human to live. But that wasn't all. God also said: "Moreover, I will give you what you have not asked for—both riches and honor" (1 Kings 3:13). The specific accounting of Solomon's wealth is found in 2 Chronicles 9:13-28. It is summed up perfectly in verse 22: "King Solomon was greater in riches and wisdom than all the other kings of the earth."

It should be noted here that neither David nor Solomon were perfect men. They were far from it. Actually between the two of them they committed some of the seemingly most abhorrent sins. David committed adultery as well as murder. Solomon had a weakness toward women and directly disobeyed God regarding them. But God's covenant was not about those things. God knows that we are human and as humans we will sin. What God wants is our hearts to be in relationship with His. This is what He honors.

Of course prosperity as a result of choosing to love God is not limited to men. In Biblical times men were the ones that made a living and provided for their families. Women kept the house and did all of the traditional things that any woman in the NOW movement would frown upon. By this fact one could surmise that for every rich and prosperous man there was also at least one rich and prosperous woman (their wives of course). Let's see, though, if we can find biblical evidence of women making a choice to serve God and as a result of that choice being rewarded with prosperity.

Ruth is the perfect example of the cause and effect relationship of loving God and receiving prosperity in return. Naomi had a husband and two sons. While in Moab, Naomi's husband had died and her two sons had married. One of the wives was none other than Ruth, a Moabitess. In an unfortunate turn of events, both of Naomi's sons also died. The three women were left alone and Naomi decided to return to Bethlehem. She tried to convince her daughters-in-law to return to their own homes. Ruth would not.

Ruth was determined to stay with Naomi and be her companion. She tells Naomi, "Don't urge me to leave you or to turn back from you. Where you go I will go, and where you stay I will stay. Your people will be my people and your God my God" (Ruth 1:6). Ruth chose to remain committed to the family that she married into. She decided to stay and aid the woman she had grown to love. But most importantly, Ruth proclaimed acceptance for the God of Israel.

After the move to Bethlehem, Ruth met a relative of Naomi's husband named Boaz. We read that Boaz was "a man of great wealth" (Ruth 2:1 NKJV). We also see from verse 4 that Boaz was a man of the Lord: "Just then, Boaz arrived from Bethlehem and greeted the harvesters, 'The Lord be with you!'" Boaz loved the Lord and Boaz was prosperous. He was so prosperous that he ends up redeeming Ruth's land and marrying her in the process. Now, I've just boiled down a very beautiful courtship and story into just a couple of paragraphs. Here is what should be taken from the above account. Ruth chose God. God allowed Ruth to be redeemed through Boaz and to share in his prosperity. Action–Reaction.

There are a number of other Old Testament saints that have this same action-reaction scenario. Instead of doing an in-depth study on each of them, I'll just list out some key Scriptures for them. This is, of course, just a sample to give you further evidence of the role that God played in the Old Testament in giving His people prosperity.

Abram: "Abram had become very wealthy in livestock and in silver and gold" (Genesis 13:2).

Isaac: "The man became rich, and his wealth continued to…" (Genesis 26:13).

Joseph: "The Lord was with Joseph and he prospered" (Genesis 39:2).

Barzillai: "…for he was a very wealthy man" (2 Samuel 19:32).

Jehoshaphat: "…he had great wealth and honor, his heart was devoted to the ways of the Lord" (2 Chronicles 17:5, 6).

Hezekiah: "…for God had given him very great riches" (2 Chronicles 32:29).

Job: "The Lord made him prosperous again, and gave him twice as much as he had" (Job 4:10).

PROSPERITY AND THE NEW TESTAMENT

It certainly is easy to find examples of people's prosperity in the Old Testament. Admittedly this is a much more daunting task for the New Testament. There are very specific reasons why it is difficult to find evidence of prosperity in the New Testament. For instance, the Old Testament is about twice as long as the New Testament. It also spans thousands of years, where the New Testament covers less than one hundred years. During the Old Testament centuries the Jews experienced their share of ups and downs. There were times of prosperity and there were times of poverty. The New Testament takes place solely in a time of unrest for the Jews. Lastly, the Old Testament is filled with books about specific people. The New Testament exclusively covers the life of Christ, the early church, or living a Christ-like life.

All that being said, it is difficult to find the biblical evidence that we are looking for in the New Testament. One could conclude that prosperity as a gift from God was solely a part of the old covenant and was not included in the new covenant. There are even some very key Scriptures that most people have heard and can recite that speak against prosperity. For instance, don't we all know that: "Money is the root of all evil," or that, "it is easier for a camel to pass through the eye of a needle than for a rich man to enter the kingdom of heaven." Now, before you jump down my throat, I purposely misquoted one of those Scriptures. How many of you know what I'm talking about?

I've often heard that money is the root of all evil. People have said this to me. I heard it so much that I actually began to believe it. It wasn't until one day I heard a preacher speak on the topic that I learned the true wording of that Scripture. Paul writes to Timothy: "For the love of money is a root of all kinds of evil" (1 Timothy 6:10). You see money is not evil. The Scripture says that the love of money is the root of different kinds of evil. Who could disagree with that statement? Just look at organized crime, drugs on the streets, and prostitution. These symbols and sins of a decadent society are all driven by the love of money. And that is undeniably evil.

The other Scripture that people use to justify this idea that a rich person can't get to heaven is when Jesus was talking to the rich young man. In Mark 10:17, the rich young man asks Jesus, "What must I do to inherit eternal life?" Jesus lists for him some of the Ten Commandments to which the man replies that he has kept them all. Jesus responds to this by telling the man to go and sell all he has, give it to the poor and follow Him. The rich young man cannot and leaves disappointed. It is at this point that Jesus tells His disciples: "Children, how hard it is to enter the kingdom of God! It is easier for a camel to go through the eye of a needle than for a rich man to enter the kingdom of God" (Mark 10:24, 25).

This Scripture has daunted Christians for ages. Does this now mean that you can't have money or wealth or possessions? I'd say that is not what Jesus is saying at all. If we read the verses around this Scripture we begin to get the idea of what Jesus was saying. First of all, we need to realize the context in which the rich young man was coming to Jesus. He obviously respected Jesus for he sought His approval. His intentions though, were not to learn what he needed to do, but to let Jesus and everyone else around know that he was a righteous man.

When Jesus listed a portion of the Ten Commandments the man instantly said that he obeyed them all. This would suggest that this man was in fact perfect. We all break the commandments. But if this man's claim is that he did not break even one of the commandments then it could be surmised that this was too easy of a task for him. Jesus responds to him by telling him, "OK, I'll accept your claim of being perfect, then it must be easy for you to obey these laws. So I'll tell you what, prove that you are worthy of the kingdom of God by doing something that won't be so easy for you. Sell all you have and follow Me." You see, the man wanted a merit-based system so Jesus gave him a merit based system. You do this – you get that.

During all of this the disciples didn't know what to think. Jesus just asked a seemingly impossible thing of the man as a requisite for eternal life. So they asked, "Who then can be saved?" (Mark 10:26). And Jesus responded with the key to our salvation in verse 27: "With man this is impossible, but not with God; all things are possible with God"

And there we have it. The whole point of the story of the rich young man is that we can try to achieve the kingdom of God by our own merits but we will always fall short. It is because of God's mercy and grace that we can have eternal life. Money was the one thing that stood in the way of this man's salvation. This man loved money more than God and that is why it was chosen as the criterion for him. God will often ask of us what we hold most dear in order to see how deep our love for Him runs.

Still though, it could be easy to say that when Jesus came, all the ways of the Old Testament were reversed. I don't find this to be the case at all. Just as Jesus spoke against the appearance of the Pharisee's adherence to the Law, Jesus spoke against the love of money. But in neither case did Jesus speak against either the Law or in having money.

We all know that the Pharisees were so obsessed with the letter of the Law that they chose to ignore the spirit of the Law. Because this was such a prevalent practice back then, Jesus often condemned the Pharisees. Nowhere did Jesus condemn the Law though. In fact in Matthew 5:17, Jesus said with regard to the Law: "I have not come to abolish them but to fulfill them."

In the time of Jesus the poor were looked down on. The Pharisees looked on prosperity solely as a gift from God. This was such the prevailing thought that it caused them to look down on the poor. The thought was that if prosperity was indeed a gift from God then lack of prosperity must be a judgment from God. Essentially, people were thought to be justified by their possessions. Jesus came and spoke against this. He came to show us that we are justified by our faith and not by the fact that we have wealth. This was the message the gospel writers were trying to get across. Once again I say, Jesus did not speak against having money. He did speak against putting money first.

I think that the most fulfilling sermon that Jesus gave with regard to material possessions is found in Matthew 6, verses 25-34. Here Jesus talks about not being concerned with material things. He says not to worry about what we will wear or what we will eat. He uses the analogy that the flowers in the field were brilliantly clothed by God and that the birds of the air didn't have to worry about storing up food and yet they are fed. Jesus tells us not to be concerned with these things and that God would provide them. He says this in a way that is like a page right out of the Old Testament's action–reaction scenario of loving God and receiving prosperity in return. We see this in verse 33: "But seek first his kingdom and his righteousness, and all these things will be given to you as well." The key is that we need to be seeking God's kingdom first.

Even toward the end of the New Testament and after Jesus had risen from the dead we see it was still understood that God wishes to prosper those who love Him. In 3 John 1:2 we read,

"I pray that you may prosper in all things and be in health just as your soul prospers" (NKJV). Therefore, as we grow closer to God (as your soul prospers) we will also prosper in all things and be in health.

EXAMPLE OF PROSPERITY IN THE NEW TESTAMENT

All that being said, let's take a look at a person in the New Testament who actually loved God and was also prosperous. The first person that comes to mind is Zacchaeus, the tax collector. Zacchaeus yearned so much for the Word of God that he actually climbed a tree to see who Jesus was and to hear Him speak. In Luke 19:2 we learn that Zacchaeus "was a chief tax collector and was wealthy." Jesus sees Zacchaeus up in the tree and instructs him to come down because He is going to Zacchaeus's house. The people were astonished and Zacchaeus was so overjoyed that he exclaimed if he ever cheated anyone he would pay them back four times what he owed and give half of his possessions to the poor. Jesus' reply to this was, "Today salvation has come to this house" (Luke 19:9).

Do you see the contrast between Zacchaeus and the rich young man? Both Zacchaeus and the rich young man were wealthy. The rich young man came to Jesus to prove he was worthy. Zacchaeus came to Jesus to grow closer to God. The rich man could not do what Jesus asked. Zacchaeus did what he was supposed to before he was even asked. The rich young man left disappointed. Zacchaeus left with Jesus, renewed, and with eternal life. It is not a matter of whether you can be rich and still love God. It is a matter of which do you love more.

GOD USES PEOPLE IN HIGH PLACES

Further support is given to the ability for an individual to have prosperity and still walk in the ways of the Lord upon examining the people that God has blessed with prosperity. God often will use the fact that a person has power, prestige, influence, and prosperity to fulfill His plan. God, in His sovereignty, will put people in these positions in order to achieve His will.

Take Joseph, Jacob's son. His brothers sold him into slavery and told Jacob that he was dead. Joseph found favor with God and therefore, through a series of orchestrated events, ended up as Pharaoh's right-hand man. Joseph was so favored that Pharaoh himself said: "You shall be in charge of my palace, and all my people are to submit to your orders. Only with respect to the throne will I be greater than you" (Genesis 41:40). God made it possible for Joseph to be able to interpret Pharaoh's dreams and gain this position of power. God then used Joseph and his influence to save up enough harvest during the seven years of prosperity to carry all of the land and the people in it through the seven years of famine to follow.

The next great Old Testament example is Esther. Esther was among the still exiled Jews in Babylon during the reign of King Xerxes. The king decided to choose a new wife and called for all of the virgins to be brought to him. Esther was so beautiful and so loved by the king that he crowned her queen out of all the women whom he met. During this time Haman, the king's most elevated official, plotted to kill all the Jews. Esther, a Jew herself, found out about this plan and prepared an elaborate scheme which involved risking her own life in order to tell the king. King Xerxes was so trusting of Haman that it would take only the words of his beloved queen to convince him of the evil that Haman was plotting. God placed Esther in the house of Xerxes in order that she might convince the king to stop Haman and prevent the Jews from annihilation.

We even find evidence of God using people of wealth to fulfill His purpose in the New Testament. Joseph of Arimathea is the focus of this example. In Matthew 27:57 we read: "As evening approached, there came a rich man from Arimathea, named Joseph, who had himself become a disciple of Jesus." After Jesus' crucifixion, Joseph requested the body of Jesus from Pilate. Joseph then took Jesus, wrapped Him in cloth, and placed Him in the tomb that was meant for him.

Now, you may be asking why this is important. The answer is simple. Because Joseph was wealthy, it gives the account credibility. We know specifically who buried Jesus. No one could legitimately argue that Jesus didn't rise from the dead for lack of a burial location. It was known by Jews and Romans alike that Jesus was buried specifically in Joseph of Arimathea's tomb. This is further evidenced by the fact that Roman guards were placed at the tomb. God chose a wealthy disciple to bury His son so that for the next 2000 years or so all would know that it was known where Jesus was buried.

CONCLUSION

We have covered a lot of ground in this chapter. We saw how the promise of prosperity in Jeremiah 29, verse 11 was a reiteration of the cause and effect relationship that the Old Testament teaches with regard to loving God and receiving prosperity. We also saw from the New Testament that wealth in itself is not evil but the choice of wealth over God is. Jesus Himself describes a cause and effect relationship between our seeking God first and our needs being fulfilled. Finally we learned of how God uses people of wealth, power, and position to carry out His plans and will for His people.

It was my intent to show that wealth and prosperity are gifts from God. We therefore should not be surprised when this happens to us, but instead be abundantly thankful for our blessings. We also need to be crystal clear about one thing: never to choose money over God. We must remember that the true prosperity we are searching for is that of our souls. One final point should be made. We never know the plans or road that God has for another believer and therefore we must not make assumptions about their wealth or lack thereof.

At this point I'd like to close this section with Paul's words to Timothy, found in First Timothy 6:17 on this very subject: "Command those who are rich in this present world not to be arrogant nor to put their hope in wealth, which is so uncertain, *but to put their hope in God, who richly provides us with everything for our enjoyment.* Command them to do good, to be rich in good deeds, and to be generous and willing to share. In this way they will lay up treasure for themselves as a firm foundation for the coming age, so that they may take hold of the life that is truly life" (Emphasis mine).

Part 2

GOD'S USE OF JEREMIAH 29 IN OUR LIVES

"For I know the plans I have for you," declares the Lord, "plans to prosper you and not to harm you, plans to give you hope and a future. Then you will call upon me and come and pray to me, and I will listen to you. You will seek me and find me when you seek me with all your heart. I will be found by you," declares the Lord, "and will bring you back from captivity. I will gather you from all the nations and places where I have banished you," declares the Lord, "and bring you back to the place from which I carried you into exile."

—Jeremiah 29:11-14

Chapter 6

BE CAREFUL WHAT YOU WISH FOR— ACHIEVING SUCCESS

"Delight yourself in the Lord and he will give you the desires of your heart."

—Psalm 37:4

Often in the pursuit of the promises of Jeremiah 29 we can lose sight of the purpose for our lives. We can become so driven that we don't even consider how what we are striving for contributes to the larger plan that God has for us. It is during these times that we are held captive to our pursuits and require God's grace to bring us back to Him. It is during these times that we end up on the different paths of life that don't allow God's plans to shine through.

We end up becoming exiled to a life that is not our own, much in the same way the Jews were exiled to Babylon. These are the times in which we need most to hear:

"For I know the plans I have for you," declares the Lord, "plans to prosper you and not to harm you, plans to give you hope and a future. Then you will call upon me and come and pray to me, and I will listen to you. You will seek me and find me when you seek me with all your heart." We need to hear this to remind us of God's promise.

God wants to bring us back even though it was our pursuit of plans that were not His that caused the troubling situation. He wants us to have good things and not to feel pain. Above all, He wants us to search for Him with all our hearts. This really is the story of my life and my inspiration for writing this book. My own personal journey has carried me to highs and lows and through it all the prophecy that is Jeremiah 29 has proved itself faithful.

I grew up in South Florida in a very religious household. I was taught to love Jesus above all else and to live out the Ten Commandments. I truly did love God and can remember spending hours as a child looking at the pictures and reading the captions of my picture Bible. I loved the stories of Daniel in the lions' den and of Joseph with his coat of many colors. I especially loved the image of Jesus playing with the children.

I attended private religious schools in South Florida through the 12th grade. This bolstered the already solid foundation of Christian beliefs that my parents and grandparents had instilled in me. It also gave me a great college preparatory education. Throughout this time I always had a solid support system consisting of my parents, grandparents, great-grandmother, sister, aunts, uncles, cousins, and friends. One could say that I lived a rather sheltered and well-protected life. God was with me every step of the way and I knew it. It was obvious that I was blessed and I was raised to never lose sight of that fact.

In 1993, I graduated from high school in the top 10% of my class. I had excelled in math and science so I decided to study Mechanical Engineering. In Chapter 1, I described how God orchestrated the next series of events to land me at Rensselaer Polytechnic Institute in Troy, NY. God placed me at RPI for the first round of tests that He would throw my way. I still remember the words my dad spoke to me as he moved me into my college dorm. He gave me one of the most loving father-son talks that anyone could hope for. The underlying theme of our discussion was, "Remember who you are, remember where you came from."

The first year of college was difficult. I felt very alone for the first time in my life. Everyone was so smart around me. I was no longer in the top of the class. I remember being faced with all kinds of temptations and choices that required a solid foundation to get through. I had eighteen years of preparation that would help me through those tough decisions and times. God also provided me with a support group of aunts and uncles nearby to help me to remember my roots (and to get a good home cooked meal on occasion).

I was able to stay true to myself, to my beliefs, and to my God for almost two years. Sometime late in my sophomore year the ways of the world began to get the better of me. I had more freedom and less responsibility than ever before and it became very easy for me to forget who I was. I had lots of friends, was well liked, and the lure of secularism was very attractive. I was also doing well in my course work. Success by all measures of society suddenly seemed very attainable whereas in the past it was always just something in the distant future.

Thankfully, by my senior year of college the pendulum had swung the other way and I was beginning to remember who I was again. I started to go back to church and to seek God's will for my life. I did, after all, have the most important decision of my life to make: the decision of where to work. God had planned and prepared me for this also. For the last eighteen months of college I had been working as a mechanical engineer at a plastic injection molding plant outside of Albany, NY. This real world experience helped me to land a job with the world's number one consumer products company, Procter & Gamble.

All of a sudden I had achieved everything I had ever worked and strived for during my life. I had a job with a great company and was making an awesome salary to go along with it. It took awhile to sink in. It felt weird to leave work and have the rest of the evening free. Up until that point I had part-time jobs or homework to do in the evening. There was no free time. Now I had all the free time I had wanted. Still though, the first few months were very much like the first few months of college. I was living in Pennsylvania and I didn't know anyone there. The situation of being alone in a new place with new responsibility helped keep me close to God. He was all that I had.

As time went on, though, things began to change similar to when I was a sophomore at RPI. I started to realize that I had money. This was a first for me. Not only did I have enough money for my bills but there was plenty left over. I had also made a lot of friends at work. This particular P&G plant was the largest in the whole company. That year they hired about 30 new managers close to my same age. We would hang out after work, go to happy hour on Friday nights, and on trips during the weekend. I became very comfortable with the life that I had and once again began losing myself.

With all the money I was making and the relatively low cost of living in Northeastern Pennsylvania I began looking for ways to use that money. Within a short period of time I had purchased a new car, a Harley Davidson motorcycle, a boat, and a time-share in Cancun. And that doesn't include all the outdoor sporting equipment that I needed for my weekend excursions. I bought such things as new kayaks, sleeping bags, backpacks, and all the necessary accompanying gear.

In addition to all the material possessions I was acquiring, my friends and I were traveling every weekend. I can barely remember a weekend when I was home. We traveled all over the Northeastern US in search of the next big party or to go white-water kayaking. We couldn't get enough travel. We wouldn't even finish one trip before we began planning another one.

But why stop with what I had? My car was no longer good enough for my activities and the trips I was planning. So I ended up buying a brand new fully loaded ¾ ton truck with an extended cab and an eight-foot box. But I wasn't finished there. I bought a truck camper for the truck to take on all those trips. About this time I figured with the bigger vehicle I could now pull a bigger boat. So I began boat shopping (again).

The materialism became like a drug to me. I always had to be researching the next big purchase or planning the next exciting trip. I was living life in the fast lane for sure. During this time, I was the furthest away from God I had ever been. My whole life I had worked hard and always done the right thing. I felt like I was enjoying the fruits of my labor, so to speak.

My personal life while at P&G was merely echoing my career at the time. From a work standpoint I got off to a bit of a rocky start. But that was soon forgotten. I built a reputation for getting the job done which began to get noticed. It wasn't long before I was routinely picked to be part of the choicest projects. High profile projects meant one thing to me—travel with friends. I was flying all over the world for Procter & Gamble. P&G sent me to Europe a few times and all over the U.S. regularly. This, of course, fit in really well with my personal life. What single guy wouldn't want to be racking up the frequent flyer miles, staying in the best hotels, renting premium vehicles, and seeing the world all on the company dollar?

By the time that I had turned 25, I was responsible for a $5 million budget and directing seventy employees. I was on video conference calls with people in three different countries. Directors in upper management knew my name. All of the accomplishments in my life became my own. I had forgotten about all the hard work and sacrifices that my parents had made to get me where I was. I had forgotten about all the prayers God answered that were the reasons I had achieved such greatness. Everything that led up to those days of success was planned and orchestrated by God. Now I was there, but I was no longer fulfilling God's plan for my life. His will was certainly secondary to my own.

If someone would have told me I wasn't fulfilling God's purpose for my life at that time I would have said he was nuts. I would have said that God was rewarding me for working so hard my whole life. I would have been mistaken. God doesn't reward us for working hard. Society might, but God doesn't. God rewards us for seeking Him with all our hearts. I had done that along the way but it certainly was an afterthought at that point. How sad for God. How betrayed He must have felt. Just think if you had a child that loved you and shared with you and was a part of so much of your life that you gave him everything he could ever need or want. Then once he received these things he no longer spent time with you or spoke to you. That is exactly what I had done to my Father, God.

So God gave me a wake-up call. I wasn't giving God the attention that He knew I was capable of so He allowed discontent to seep into my life. It was rather suddenly actually. Through no fault of my own, a project I was working on began to hit some obstacles. Days began to run together. Seventy-hour work weeks became the norm. On more than one occasion I would have my car packed for the weekend only to realize on Friday night that I wasn't able to go anywhere. One day I went into work at 6 A.M. and I didn't end up leaving until 6 P.M. the next day. I worked 36 straight hours, only catching a one-hour nap at my desk from 3 A.M. to 4 A.M. I was no longer in control. This went on for about a year.

I began questioning what it was I was doing with my life. What was my purpose? Was I to waste away in a manufacturing plant? What was this drive and need that I had to get ahead? At about this time I was able to squeeze a couple days of vacation to meet my family at a beach house in Northern Florida for Memorial Day. I decided to drive. I needed to clear my head and driving was a great way for me to do that. On the way down I was really looking for answers. I don't remember how much I prayed but I do remember that I didn't know what I was going to do.

When I arrived at the beach I was very distant with my family. My parents couldn't wait to hear how things were going. I just couldn't relate to them. How do you tell your parents who helped you achieve everything you had ever prayed and worked for that you aren't happy? I ended up hanging out in a beach chair with a six-pack of beer and staying very distant from my family. One night my mother literally cornered me in the cabin and started to cry. She told me that she was worried about me and that my father missed having me as a friend. I was heartbroken. Not only was my relationship with myself in poor shape but it began to affect my relationship with my family.

There is a trio of relationships that each of us has. They are your relationship with yourself, your relationship with others, and your relationship with God. It is a cycle. Each is like a link on chain. If one of those links is broken the connection is lost and the chain is broken. In my life the cycle begins with God. When my relationship with God falters, so does my ability to be happy in life. I become discontented and regretful. When I am not happy with myself, I am unable to relate to others. The only thing to do is to mend the relationship with God and to get the chain working again.

Jesus spoke of this trio of relationships when He was asked what the most important commandment was. Jesus' reply was: "Love the Lord your God with all your heart and with all your soul and with all your mind. This is the first and greatest commandment. And the second is like it: Love your neighbor as yourself. All the Law and the Prophets hang on these two commandments" (Matthew 22:37-40). It is even ordered for us. We must first have a relationship with God. The second commandment implies that we must love both our neighbor and ourselves, but before we can love our neighbor we must first love ourselves.

My whole life I had wanted success and wealth. I had prayed for it and worked for it. God in return granted it. The problem was that I failed to give glory to the Source of all of the blessings. It brings to mind a lesson that Jesus taught regarding this very issue. In Matthew 16:26 Jesus says, "What good will it be for a man if he gains the whole world, yet he forfeits his soul." I never intended to lose my soul. But I essentially chose position and power over love of the Lord. I'm just glad that He chose to bring me back to Him.

There are many different reasons God allows Christians to go through tough times. One reason is that He wants our attention. Sometimes this is the only way to get it. Now I'm not saying that God causes bad things to happen. I'm not saying that at all. What I am saying is that God does allow them to happen. He then will use the bad things to bring us back to Him.

In my case God allowed me to make my own choices and to choose to gain power and success at work. I vied so much for these things that I became noticed. I was so noticed that I was placed in high profile positions. These were the same positions that required much attention, time, and responsibility. He allowed all of this to happen. He then used the resulting discontentment in my life to bring me back to Him. I wish that it didn't play out like that. I really do. I wished that I could have turned to the Lord much earlier and that it didn't take an unhappy situation to bring me back. But I can't change that now. I can only be thankful to God for not just bringing me back to Him but for actually wanting me back.

Chapter 7

WORSE BEFORE
BETTER

"When you pass through the waters, I will be with you; and when you pass through the rivers they will not sweep over you. When you walk through the fire, you will not be burned; the flames will not set you ablaze"

—Isaiah 43:2

It was obvious that I had to make a change. I was lost in the world that was my life. I hated work. I couldn't relate to family. It even became difficult to deal with my friends. Since many of my best friends were assigned to the same projects as I, they were feeling the same pressures and stresses I had felt. Our conversations became consumed with the problems of work and there seemed to be no escape.

I know you may be thinking that the problems that I am describing really weren't that bad. "I mean, come on, George. You're working a dream job, making a lot of money, and have tons of friends." Well you'd be right in a lot of respects. By society's standards I was better off than over 95% of the world. That is not the point at all. By God's standards I had lost my soul. I was not fulfilling His purpose for me. I may have been a productive member of society but I was not a productive member of the family of God.

On the drive back from Florida I did a lot of thinking and praying. It became as clear as the light of day. I needed to make a change. It was not that I thought I should make a change; I knew that I had to make a change. God made this perfectly certain in my mind. For the months leading up to this point I was unsure about what I was going to do. It was on this drive that I began to seek God's plan for me.

Growing up I had always wanted to become a teacher. I wanted to be able to influence others in the same way that my teachers had influenced me. The reason that I decided to study engineering was because it would give me more options and it was considered a successful career. On the drive back home I decided to go back to that high school dream and become a high school math teacher.

In addition to realizing that I needed to change careers, that trip also made me realize something I wasn't previously aware of. I had grown distant from all the people who meant so much to me. This awakening led me to the decision that I would move back home. I finally had a concrete goal to be running toward instead of merely running away from my life. You see, the plan that God has for us doesn't involve taking us from one inadequate path to another equally useless path. God's plans give us purpose, meaning, and fulfill our lives. We want to work toward them. We feel pride in fulfilling them. I thank God for having them.

And thus began the journey home. Coincidently, Procter & Gamble was offering voluntary separation packages to those that wished to leave the company. They were looking to downsize and didn't believe in layoffs. In June I signed one the packages and we came upon the agreement that I would not leave until January. God was starting to make things happen. My life was changing for the better. Everything was going to be all right. Or so I thought.

Just because you follow God's will for your life, it doesn't mean there won't be bumps along the way. I had to learn this the hard way. For a couple months everything was fine. Work wasn't too bad since there was an end in sight. A lot of the pressure and stress was relieved just by the fact it was known that I was leaving in a few months. The company had to assign other employees to handle the longer-term issues. But there were other obstacles to overcome.

I had to tell my parents I was quitting my job, which would be anything but easy. My dad was in the Catskill Mountains of New York in August of 2001 for a vacation. I figured that was as good a time as any to let him know what I was going to do. We were walking on a quiet road enjoying the scenery and splendor of the surrounding nature when I decided to break the news. To say that he wasn't happy would be an understatement. Now before you get the wrong idea about the discussion, I should say that there was no yelling or anything like that. It was just this sense I got that he was disappointed in me for quitting.

My family was always so proud I had worked as hard as I did and was making it on my own. It made them feel good to be able to say that their son was a mechanical engineer and a manager with Procter & Gamble. They knew that I not only had a great career but I also had a secure job. This was important to them.

The conversation with my father left me with some major doubts about what I was about to do. Was I really throwing it all away? Why don't I stay in engineering and get a job with a different company? Would I be able to live on a teacher's salary after being so accustomed to having and spending money at will? These questions coursed through my mind and left me wondering whether I had done the right thing or not.

The next major blow came in September of 2001. Before you jump to any conclusions about 9/11, that is not what I am talking about. I was on a business trip in Cincinnati when this setback transpired. One night I was taking a walk and passed by a sand volleyball court. It instantly reminded me of my good friend, Mike, with whom I had grown up. We would play volleyball for hours on the beach in Hollywood, FL. It occurred to me that I hadn't spoken with him for a while. He had no idea that I was going to move back home. I figured that I'd give him a call in a day or so and tell him the good news.

The next day at the work site I was visiting I received one of the most harrowing calls of my life. It was my mother. Something was obviously wrong. She told me that someone I was close to was in a car accident and didn't make it. She was talking about Mike. Instantly denial came over me. That was impossible. Mike couldn't be dead. I was just thinking about him the night before. He had a four-month-old baby and a new wife. How could he be dead? As it sank in, I collected myself and booked a ticket to go back home for the funeral. It was not going to be the homecoming that I'd been long awaiting.

The next day was September 11, 2001, and we all know how history changed that day. As we were being attacked all I could think about was Mike. As the towers fell I stood crying about Mike. It was the single most significant day I'd ever witnessed in our nation's history and I was utterly consumed with thoughts of my good friend, Mike. It never occurred to me what the repercussions of the terrorist attacks would be on our world. I was more concerned with whether or not my flight would be cancelled.

Well of course I couldn't make my way back to Florida for the funeral. I was by myself in a strange place knowing almost no one and our country was under attack. I'd never felt so alone in my entire life. I just kept wondering why all of this was happening and where I had gone wrong. And of course I couldn't keep myself from thinking: Why hadn't I just called Mike two days before when I was thinking of him?

I remember driving while looking for gas and feeling totally lost. What had my life become? Why couldn't I be happy? I thought I was making changes in my life for the better. I thought I was past the hard part already. But the obstacles just kept popping up. Where was God?

It turns out that God was right where He was supposed to be. Of course God knew of the events that would take place long before they ever did. He knew that I'd be feeling lost and alone at that very moment and He had planned for it. He actually positioned me from weeks before to be able to handle those circumstances. When I was booking the work trip to Cincinnati He put it in my head that I should go and visit my old theology teacher and high school cross-country coach, Scott McDade. Scott was my teacher and friend. But as with many of my relationships we had grown apart. Well, for some reason I had the big idea that I should visit him in San Francisco at the end of that business trip. So I booked a layover in California on the way home from Cincinnati weeks before I even took the trip. God had planted the seed in my head knowing that I would need to be with a friend who could relate to my pain.

Well the day that I was supposed to go to San Francisco had arrived and only a few airports had reopened. As it turned out my flight out was one of the first planes to go back up into the sky after the attacks. I wasn't concerned at all with safety. I just wanted to see a familiar face and to be with my friend. I had missed the funeral. The best way for me to commemorate the life of Mike was to spend it with our mutual friend and former cross-country coach. So I got on that plane and headed to California.

On that trip I reconnected with an old mentor and friend. We reminisced about Mike and the memories we had. We talked about what was important in life. It became clear to me that all the events I had looked at as obstacles in the way of my happiness were actually events in support of the decision I had made. The life that I was leading was a result of years of neglecting the relationships that had meant so much to me. I couldn't relate to my dad and I hadn't spoken with my friends. These difficulties were just the ripple effects of my previous behavior, not reflections of my current decisions.

God used all of these obstacles to help me grow. He planned each day before I was born. This is an extremely hard concept for us to grasp. In Psalm 139, verse 16 we read: "All the days ordained for me were written in your book before one of them came to be." Some people may even be upset reading this. I find comfort in it. I love the fact that my Father in heaven knew that I would go through tough times and planned a way for me to deal with them. I had traveled over 100,000 miles during those years. Yet, I never once thought of going to see McDade until that trip. The Holy Spirit planted that seed in my mind a whole month before Mike passed away. That visit became the single most unifying moment of my decision to seek God's will for me. It was the affirmation that I needed to know what I was doing was right.

January came and 2002 started off with tons of excitement. I sold my truck. I sold my camper. I sold my boat. I sold my exercise equipment. I even sold my 8-foot boa. I bought an old cargo van and trailer, packed them full, and moved back to Florida. I felt so alive on that drive back home. The possibilities were endless in my mind. Upon arrival in the Sunshine State, my parents' excitement reached heights that equaled mine. They were really just excited that I'd be living at home once again.

The plan was this. I was going to find a job at a restaurant somewhere. I'd also help manage my parent's business. All the money I had received from Procter & Gamble's separation package was spent paying off credit card bills and loans I had accumulated. I was basically broke. I would need to earn enough money from February through May to be able to take off in June and July and travel around the country. I would, in the meantime, apply for teaching jobs and hopefully start work in August of that year.

It seemed easy enough. I found a job at a South Beach restaurant that was about to open. That and the time I would be putting in at my parents' business should gain me enough to take my summer trip. I would be living with my parents so my expenses would be drastically cut from what they were. In addition, the girl I had been dating in Cincinnati had planned to move down to Florida and get a place. We were going to stay together and she was looking forward to the relocation. I really thought I was past the tough part and it would be smooth sailing from there on out.

Well, once again I was wrong. The restaurant that hired me ended up having their licenses delayed for about a month. That was one less month of money for me to put in the bank. But that was the least of my worries. The next hurdle to overcome was a pretty scary one actually. I had begun to feel this burning sensation low in my chest. The pain was persistent and after a week of thinking it would go away, I became worried. At this same time I received a denial letter for a life insurance policy that I had applied for. The reason was because there were traces of blood in my urine.

Between the burning chest and the bloody urine I figured that I'd better go to the doctor. Of course since I was in between jobs my health insurance was far from stellar. I was able to get some COBRA coverage when I left P&G but since I moved out of state the coverage was spotty at best. I'm just glad that I decided to take it. I figured that regardless of the cost, I'd better get checked out. Well, it was a good thing that I did. I ended up finding out that I had an ulcer. But that wasn't all. I also had kidney stones. All of the stress of trying to climb the corporate ladder had finally taken its toll. Like my damaged relationships, this was yet another problem that manifested itself long after it was caused.

The medication and doctor bills began to pile up but at least I had gotten help and was being treated. Still, my prospects were beginning to look bleak for my summer excursion; I wasn't saving up nearly enough money. The restaurant didn't have the kind of opening they were expecting. On some days I spent more money on gas, tolls, and parking than I received in tips. As all of this was going on I found out that the girl that I had been dating decided she couldn't make the move to Florida after all. And then to top it all off, my van needed a new radiator—another bill to pay.

My dreams of taking a two-month trip were fading away fast. I had always dreamed of hitting the road with all my gear and just throwing caution to the wind. I was never able to take time off between high school and college or between college and starting my job. I figured that this would be the best chance to live out this dream before I started yet another job. But all of that just seemed like an impractical notion at this point. I once again began to doubt the decision to leave the security of my old job in search of a better life. My perceived problems at P&G were nothing compared to what I was dealing with back in Florida.

I once again began to seek God with my heart. Somehow I had forgotten and once again I had reason to seek. I prayed and asked God to heal my ulcer and to remove my kidney stones. I prayed that I would get over my girlfriend. I prayed for my finances. I acknowledged that these were my wishes. I then prayed for God's will for my life and not my own.

As with my last set of trials God was right there with me. He sent me two signs that clearly gave me the message that I was doing what I needed and should stay the course. The first message that He sent me was my good friend, Web. Web had been one of my P&G buddies who I had grown extremely close to. It makes me laugh how these next events transpired. I was dealing with the ulcer, the kidney stones, the bills, the broken relationship, and working the two jobs all while just trying to make ends meet when Web called. He wanted to pay me a visit. I told him it wasn't a good time. I just needed to focus on working and staying healthy. I didn't have time for him. The pattern seemed to start all over again. I move. I get busy. I lose relationships.

Well, Web didn't accept my words. He just kept calling and telling me of his plans to visit. He pretended that he didn't even hear me. I kept reiterating my words that I was too busy for a visit. He just kept saying that he was coming. Well, he eventually did come down. He said he knew that things were rough for me and he felt like he should be with me. Wow! Now that's friendship. God sent Web as a reminder to me of the importance of relationships. I am eternally grateful to Web for making the trip and to God for sending him to me.

The next news provided another great boost for me. I had sent a résumé and letter to my old high school inquiring about a teaching position and they called me for an interview. I was so overjoyed when I walked on the campus to see some of the same faces that were there ten years before. I was even interviewed by people I knew at the school from my senior year there. They gave me the job on the spot. The most difficult part of the move to Florida was now taken care of. What better place to begin my teaching career than at my alma mater?

Finally things were going smoothly. I remembered why I was making the career change and move. My health was getting better. And I had a job to look forward to in August. I'm still not sure how the finances worked out but when May came around it looked like I had saved up enough money to take the trip. That was yet another gift from God, no doubt.

Well, the week before my anticipated departure I was tested one more time. I figured what could go wrong now. I was healthy. I had stored up enough money for the trip. Web was even going to come with me for two of the weeks. And I had a job to come back home to in two months. Everything was setup perfectly. And as if on cue, the water pump on my van began to leak. My van was the last piece in the puzzle to enable me to live out this dream. I would be packing it full of gear. Kayaks would be on the roof and mountain bikes would be hanging off the back. There was a couch inside to sleep on. If I had no van, I had no trip.

I had come too far to just give up on the eve of the greatest trip of my life. I decided to go anyway. A leaky water pump was the least of my worries with the van. All kinds of things were rattling and it was always threatening to overheat. I wasn't about to dump another dime into it. I was going to take the chance and make the trip anyway. I know this sounds crazy. It sure did to my dad. But I had had enough. Nothing was going to stop me. I decided to bring the van's title with me. If it broke down, I'd have it towed to a junkyard and sign it over. I would them rent an SUV and drive back home. I was going to take that trip.

As I think back on those times, I gain some extremely valuable lessons. I had already realized that I needed to make a change and I took the step to do so. But taking that step in seeking God's will for me didn't preclude me from having to go through more trials. It was actually during this time that I had more obstacles than ever before. I endured a broken relationship with my parents, the death of my friend, an ulcer, kidney stones, medical bills, automobile bills, a poor job, and the breakup with my girlfriend. This was far more to deal with than the mere discontent I felt while at P&G.

Most of the trials were actually the ripple effect of the life I was leading prior to the change. You see, making a change does not erase all of our prior actions. Things were set in motion well before they actually manifested themselves. The mere acceptance of the fact that a change would be necessary is in no way able to stop the domino effect that was already in place. The failed relationships and medical issues and even the lack of money were all side effects of my former life that would need to play out.

In going through these tests of will I learned one key element of how God works. God loves us so much. He really does. And He knows what trials will befall us before they actually do. He actually permits them to happen. But He doesn't just sit by and watch things play out. He sends us His Spirit. His Spirit directs our actions and the actions of those around us, even months in advance, all to position us so that we have the tools we need to deal with the circumstances. The Spirit guided me to book that ticket to see McDade in California before Mike died. God sent Web to visit me when I was feeling low and questioning my choices. God put it in me to apply for a job with my alma mater in an effort to position me in a familiar environment and to let me know that the plan was being fulfilled.

Another amazing lesson I learned about God is how He derives pleasure from our happiness. Still to this day, I'm amazed at how God worked it out for me to take that six-week trip around the country. It was my plan. It was my desire. It was to serve my purposes. Yet God worked the whole thing out for me. He orchestrated all the necessary events so that I could take that trip.

He knew I wanted it and it was my reward for following His will. It was His pleasure since I sought Him with all my heart. He brought me out of my captivity. He told me to wait just a bit longer than I wanted. He told me that He had plans for me. Then He showed me just how great they would be.

Chapter 8

OUR PLANS VS. GOD'S PLANS

"No eye has seen, no ear has heard, no mind has conceived what
God has prepared for those who love him."

—1 Corinthians 2:9

Imagine that you are hiking on a mountain in the woods. You see a clearing up ahead. It's what you have been working toward all along. You fell along the way. On two occasions you took a wrong turn and ended up having to backtrack. But now you're here. So you take the last step up and push the branches aside. The anticipation is killing you. What comes next is truly breathtaking. You have arrived at a lookout over some rugged cliffs. There is an eagle soaring overhead and some deer in the valley below. You snap some pictures, enjoy the scenery, and relish the moment. Now that you've reached your destination—the one you set for yourself—and daylight is running out you decide to turn back.

But wait. What's this? You see that the path goes on. Do you follow it? But this wasn't a part of the plan and it surely wasn't on the map. Yet there it is. As you look down the trail you realize the path is not without risk. It is narrow and steep, not to mention that daylight is running out. It doesn't take much deliberation as the suspense is killing you. You decide to press on and after dealing with some downed trees and a couple of detours around a few creeks you come to a huge clearing with a 360-degree view of the mountains above and valleys below. It is far more magnificent than what you had expected or even planned on seeing. Had you not chosen to press on past your comfort zone and beyond your plan you would have missed it altogether.

Perhaps if you're a hiker you've experienced to some degree what I just described. Countless times I've been on hikes while trying to follow a map or a trail. I would arrive at what I perceived as my planned destination such as a waterfall or an overlook only to realize that a surprise awaited just a bit further down the trail.

Once while on a hike I had done a number of times before, I decided to go just a bit further. The path became dense and overgrown. It was obvious that most people had turned back long before. But I pressed on and literally pushed back a branch to find a downed airplane. Now granted, the plane had probably crashed decades before but it was the coolest thing I had ever seen. Had I decided to only go as far as I was used to going I would have missed that experience altogether.

That metaphor is similar to the plans God has for our lives. We may think we have attained some level of success or achieved our goal but it pales in comparison to what is just around the bend. It just requires us to take the next step. We need to push past our comfort zone. We need to say yes unconditionally to God.

THE PLANS WE MAKE AND GOD'S PLANS FOR US

We are human, so we plan. We have a desired outcome in mind and we set out to achieve it. As an engineer I had been trained in problem solving and so I approach most of the goals in my life as problems to be solved. I even approach God's work in this way. I envision the end result and plan accordingly. Pray, Plan, Act, Reflect, Pray, Plan, Act, Reflect. The cycle continues until the work is done or the goal is achieved. The funny thing is that every time I plan and then execute the plan the end result is far greater than what I set out to achieve.

Until just recently I had my great-grandmother around. She was as sharp as a whip even up to her last months on this earth. Grandma Nadima was known for her cooking and, boy, was it good. My interactions and conversations with my great-grandmother were usually centered on the Syrian specialties that she would cook and how delicious they were, or on quick little expressions of joy and affection. When she was in her seventies and I was just a boy I'd tell her, "In ten years you're still going to be making me grape leaves for dinner." She would usually respond with "Ten years? No, no...too much." Then when I was a teenager and she was in her eighties we would recycle the same conversation. No one officially knew how old she was when the Lord took her but it is estimated she was in her mid- to upper nineties.

A couple of years ago it was starting to become obvious that there wasn't going to be another "Ten years." I prayed that God would keep her comfortable and to show me what I could do for her. I decided to spend as much time with my Grandma Nadima as I could to keep her company and to keep her spirits up. So I visited her in the hospital and again a few times when she was home. We talked and joked. She told me about the days when she came to this country and when she was married—all when she was barely a teenager.

When she died I felt happy I had given her that opportunity. Then it became apparent that even though the goal was to keep her company, the outcome was far greater. I ended up learning so much about my family's past. I learned and felt the love that she had for me even though I was only one out of about 40 or 50 of her grandchildren and great-grandchildren (she knew exactly how many and could name each one). I saw firsthand how God works in the life of a praying person. I saw and felt a peace that words cannot describe.

This cycle has played out over the last few years on the retreat program that I am a part of at our school also. During my second year as a teacher I was invited to attend the school's Encounter Program, a four-day retreat for 11th and 12th graders. I was just supposed to go and hang out with the students while the adults and student leaders had meetings during the days.

I prayed that God would help me set the right example. I planned the talk that I was to give at the end of the four days. I put the plans into action as I shared at different times during the retreat. Then I reflected on the experience when it was all done. I realized that I went in with the idea I would be doing something good for the students but the end result was much greater. God had started to work in my life again during that Encounter Retreat in 2003.

God's plans are totally inconceivable to the planning mind. The engineer in me wrestles with this. As I touched on before, I like to make plans and stick to them. I need to consider, think out, rationalize, and plan every detail. It's what I was trained to do. It's what I was paid to do. It is lucky for me that my explorer instincts are more dominant than my engineering instincts. For as long as I can remember I liked to explore, to chart new territory, to take risks, and to come out ahead. It is the explorer in me that allows me to take Jeremiah 29 to heart, to look forward to the plans God has for me, to enjoy the journey en route to achieving those plans, and to always be ready for the surprises that unfold along the way.

When God led me to leave Procter & Gamble I was excited. It was going to be an adventure and a challenge. I was going into the realm of the unknown. I planned it out to perfection. As we've already seen, there were definitely bumps along the way but the sequence of events played out pretty smoothly. I quit P&G in January. In April I secured a job for August. I made enough money to take my summer trip. I then started my new job, just as planned, in August. God was with me every step of the way and I learned invaluable lessons about the faithfulness of God through the trials that I faced.

But once I started working in August I thought that was it. I was going to coast for a while. The plan at that point was to work toward my full-time teaching certificate during the year and then travel during the winter, spring, and summer breaks. That was it. I didn't think past getting the job but God sure did. God's plans for me were so much greater than my own. The funny thing is that had I known the plans going in I probably wouldn't have been so thrilled with the idea.

I had a remarkably smooth transition to the new career. I was 27 years old and the kids seemed happy to have a new young face around the school. I was also coaching the cross-country team at the time, which got me right into the swing of things around campus. Teaching came pretty easily to me, also. The engineering courses I was used to made high school math seem elementary. I'd be lying if I said that classroom management was easy, though. All in all I had a relatively smooth year and had settled in nicely to this career change.

My plans had played out perfectly and I was looking forward to another summer of travel. I am using the words *my plans* deliberately here. The events that took place were actually God's plans for my life but there was so much more to them that I didn't know about. The way I saw it, God had led me to move back to Florida to be near family and to utilize my career skills as a teacher. I had done both of those things. I had no other signs of what to do next, so I naturally assumed that the plans were fulfilled. I had achieved the destinations on my journey and that was it. Right? Wrong. God's plans had merely just begun to play out.

At this point God chose to affirm the steps I had taken before He was going to ask me to go a little further. There were two things I had set out to accomplish. The first was to move back to Florida. The next was to get a job as a high school math teacher. I had achieved both. Those achievements could have been considered all of the affirmation that I needed. But God wanted to leave me no doubt. How awesome is that! God wants to let us know He is pleased with us. So He sent me opportunities and signs to prove it.

The evidence for my move back to Florida mounted an overwhelming defense for the position that I had done the right thing. I was not aware of all I had missed by being away for the last ten years. I was given opportunities to make up for it. First, I was able to become a part of my parents' lives again. I was having meals with them and spending time with them. I proved to be a big help in their business, which served to give them the much-needed time off they rarely got. That first year I moved home it happened to be my parent's 30th anniversary. Due to the constraints of the business they were always forced to take separate vacations. As an anniversary present to them I managed their business for over a week in the summer, cutting into my own trip, so they could actually take a vacation together to commemorate this event.

The next gift granted was that I was able to be a part of the planning of my grandparents' 50th anniversary party. I am one of the few adults blessed enough to have one full set of grandparents still alive and very productive. By being away I had missed out on valuable time with them. By being back home I was able to plan for them and be with them on this awesome milestone.

There were a number of other events and happenings that I was able to share in by being back home. I was able to plan and put on my mother's surprise 50th birthday party. Two years later I did the same for my father's surprise 60th birthday. Yes, they really are that far apart in age. And I already told you about the time I was able to spend with my great-grandmother before the Lord took her. I look at the role I was able to have in all of these events as a direct sign from God that I had made the right choice to move back home and I was right where I was supposed to be.

On the career level I was given equally compelling signs in support of the change. Only halfway through my second year of teaching I was awarded Teacher of the Year by my school for a local award. What made this award especially meaningful to me was that it was chosen by the students. The administration then put their stamp of approval on my nomination. I was very humbled by the fact that not only did my employer approve of my work but also the students, who were the reason I was there, felt value in having me teach them.

It was right at this time that I began to internalize Jeremiah 29, verse 11. One Sunday at my parent's house, my grandfather pulled me aside and said he wanted to read something to me. He read: "For I know the plans I have for you," declares the Lord, "plans to prosper you and not to harm you, plans to give you hope and a future. Then you will call upon me and come and pray to me, and I will listen to you. You will seek me and find me when you seek me with all your heart" (Jeremiah 29:11-13).

I had seen the Scripture before. It was framed in my father's office at work. But it was here that I began to apply it to my life. When my grandfather read this to me I really began to think. I took those words as God saying that I had fulfilled His plans for me. I took those words as yet another affirmation that I had done what I was supposed to do. It wasn't until later that I understood my grandfather was giving me a message directly from God about my future and not about my past.

I started to realize that I had been living out God's plans but that something was missing. I believed in God. I prayed to God. I trusted in God. All of that was enough to get me where I was. But something was missing. I wasn't seeking God with all of my heart. Jeremiah 29 and the Encounter Retreats that I went on as a guest made me realize that I needed to do more. I realized that I needed to work on seeking God and on loving God. I needed to work on truly loving God with all my heart.

God was preparing me for a whole new series of events, the first of which was He asked me to become a more permanent part of the Encounter Program at our school. I had gone a few times as a guest teacher but now I was asked to take a permanent role in the program. This would require going on four of these four-day retreats each year. It would also require training students to be leaders for each one. I accepted without even giving it a second thought. I couldn't help but think this was the true reason God brought me home.

The next thing that happened came as a surprise to me. An opening came up in school administration. I really had never thought about being a part of administration since I was happy enough teaching. I truthfully wasn't looking for more responsibility either. But God put the bug in my ear to put in for the job, so I did. I ended up landing the job and becoming the new Director of Admissions of the school. In addition to my new responsibilities I would continue to teach and be an adult leader on the four Encounter retreats each year.

God handpicked me for each of these positions. He prepared me for His plans well in advance of letting me know what they were. I'm really glad He did. If God had told me some of His plans while I was still discontented at Procter & Gamble I probably would have been less than excited about them. He gradually worked me into it while preparing me along the way. And once again the end result was far greater than I had ever planned.

And even then I thought the plans were fulfilled. I thought: "Wow! My life has meaning. My life has purpose. Surely this is the plan God has for me." And it was. But that wasn't all. God had yet one more surprise for me. It was the last thing in the world I had ever expected. I certainly wasn't looking for what happened next. God gave me a wife.

I know that most people's plans include finding their significant other. They want that special someone with whom to live out their days here on earth. Well, not me. I had been soured by relationships of the past. I had seen what so-called committed married people do at the first chance they get away. I witnessed first hand an inordinate amount of men and women alike while on business travel, away from their spouses, and breaking their marriage vows only to return home to their loved ones as if nothing had happened. Furthermore, I have seen my fair share of people who settled on their choice of spouse for fear of being alone. I can recall a discussion that I had with a friend who told me she didn't want to be old and alone. To this I swiftly replied, "I'd rather be alone and lonely than miserably married."

Well, God couldn't have a member of His family having this kind of attitude about one of the purest institutions He created. So He decided to shake things up a bit. He started laying the groundwork during the same year I was named Teacher of the Year, Assistant Encounter Director, and Director of Admissions. In the midst of all that He threw Susan into my life. It's quite an amazing story actually.

Susan and I had gone to high school together. We didn't know each other to well but during our senior year we sat next to each other during one of our classes. It was during this class that we bonded. I ended up getting a "C" that year due to the distraction in the desk next to me. I also used to see Susan rollerblading on the beach while I was playing volleyball. I was highly attracted to her but very shy about my intentions. The last time I had seen Susan was at graduation. I hadn't heard from her that whole time from May of 1993 to November of 2003.

It was actually the weekend of our ten-year reunion when we were reunited. The coincidence of it is that neither of us was going to the reunion. I figured I already kept in touch with everyone I had wanted to, so why should I go. She figured the same. Well, randomly in the city of Fort Lauderdale at a complex known as Riverfront, we ran into each other that Thanksgiving weekend. I had been to this waterfront plaza dozens of times before yet had never stumbled upon Susan. But on that weekend of our ten-year reunion that neither of us was planning to attend, our eyes met.

The greeting and excitement was mutual. We began to talk for a while and I even asked for her phone number. I told her I was a teacher at our old high school and that I loved it. When it came time to part I asked if I could call her and she responded yes. I wasn't so sure about the tone of the "yes" response. Well, I ended up not calling her. I actually told myself that I would, but one day turned to two, which turned into a week. The truth was I really didn't want to be in a relationship. I liked the way my life was going and didn't want to change it.

Well, my neglect couldn't overpower Susan's determination. She didn't have my phone number but she had the next best thing. She knew where I worked. Susan ended up finding out my email address and sent me an email. It was a very friendly and unassuming note. I couldn't believe it. Of course I couldn't neglect that and I mailed her back. A couple of notes turned into a phone call which led to a date and the rest was history.

I ended up going on a ski trip for about two weeks for the New Year. I never expected the relationship to last past that trip, but it did. And after a couple of months I realized that

Susan and I had something really special. She met my family and I met hers. We were both pleasantly surprised. But then I did something I had never done with a girl before. I began to seek God with Susan. We went to see *The Passion of the Christ* together after which we had some really good discussions. Next, we read aloud *More Than A Carpenter* by Josh McDowell. We both began seeking God with all of our hearts and searched for His will for us.

It didn't take long before I knew that Susan and I were meant to be together. After eight months of dating I took Susan on a trip to the Catskill Mountains. She thought we were going camping. The very same day we got there we hiked up to Sunset Rock above North and South Lake Park. It was while we were sitting on top of Sunset Rock that I presented her with the ring and the proposal. Four months later we were married. The entire courtship up until the point where we said our vows took less than one year. When you know, you know.

Through my journey I have realized one thing. God's plans will always be better than my own. I remember when the plan was to move to Florida and teach. Once that happened I never could have expected or even imagined being named Teacher of the Year, Assistant Encounter Director, Director of Admissions, or finding a wife all in the same twelve-month span. I have learned to expect the unexpected. I look forward to the surprises and grow closer to God with every one.

As I look back on this journey I also reflect on those words my grandfather read to me that afternoon in my parents' living room: "For I know the plans I have for you," declares the Lord, "plans to prosper you and not to harm you, plans to give you hope and a future. Then you will call upon me and come and pray to me, and I will listen to you. You will seek me and find me when you seek me with all your heart" (Jeremiah 29:11-13). Those words were and are still a prophecy of my future and not a summary of my past. Praise be to God!

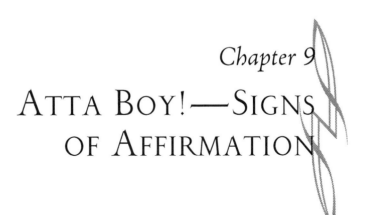

Chapter 9
ATTA BOY!—SIGNS
OF AFFIRMATION

"Therefore the Lord himself will give you a sign"
—Isaiah 7:14 NIV

The question that I often get asked by people is, "How do you know whether or not you are doing what God wants you to do?" I tell them that the answer is simple. God will give you signs in your life that you are right where you need to be and doing exactly what you are supposed to be doing. This has proven itself in my life time and again.

In Chapter 1, "Doors Will be Opened", we learned how God leads us in the direction He wishes us to go. He opens doors for us to help show us the way. Sometimes it is easier to realize these signs in hindsight rather than when they are happening. Then when things are going well and the job is finished we look back and realize how obvious the decision should have been at the time it was made. Hindsight is, indeed, twenty-twenty.

But what about when we're well on our way to following what we perceive as God's plan for our life? What then? How do you know whether or not you made the right decision? How do you know if you are doing what you are supposed to be doing? It is during these times that God will give us signs of affirmation to let us know we are doing exactly what we are supposed to be doing and we are right where we are supposed to be. In Chapter 7, "Worse before Better", I showed how it was during these times God strategically used people to help me through the obstacles and indicate to me that I needed to forge on and stay the course.

So, up until this point we've covered two ways in which God lets us know what He is thinking. The first is He opens doors for us that were previously closed. The next is He will place people in our lives to be support for us and help direct us through the obstacles. There is a third way that God lets us know we are following His will for us. This is perhaps the coolest way yet. It goes directly back to Jeremiah 29 and the plans God has to prosper you. God grants us signs of affirmation. He gives us earthly rewards to let us know we are on the right track.

I say this is cool because it amazes me. God doesn't have to reward us. He chooses to reward us. Remember, God is sovereign. He can do what He wants, when He wants. But He loves us so much that He chooses to reward us and in the process He ends up affirming what we already feel in our hearts. He lets us know He is pleased with us.

When I made the decision to leave Procter & Gamble I naturally thought things would be just fine. I then went through the most trying year of my life. Once everything began to settle down and I started teaching high school, things were great. I loved teaching the kids math and coaching the cross-country team. For the first time in a long while, I was really happy with my life.

It didn't take long for me to feel I had made the right decision to follow my heart. I traveled across the country again the summer following my first year of teaching. As the second year, began I was even more comfortable as a teacher and classroom management became much easier. I was fully settled into my new life of traveling during the breaks, working with teens as my job, and being with family and friends the rest of the time. I could have relied solely on my heart to tell me I was following God's will for my life. Deep down in my heart I felt the satisfaction. There was a calm there that I had not known for a long time. God spoke to my heart as a sign of His pleasure in me. He gave me the kind of peace that the Old Testament speaks about.

God truly could have stopped there. I was utterly and magnificently happy. I couldn't have asked for anything more for my life and I was convinced that I was leading the life God had for me. But all of that was just a feeling. Feelings can leave just as easily as they come to us. It's easy to feel as if we're doing God's will when there is no adversity in our lives. But what do we do and think when things aren't going so well? So just to make sure I was clear on His pleasure, God decided to reward me. He decided to give me a physical sign of the affirmation that He placed in my heart.

It was at this time that I had won Teacher of the Year. I was halfway through my second year of teaching when the principal told me. I couldn't believe it. I remember thinking, "How can this be?" I was brand new to the profession and only had one full year under my belt. Yet the students voted and the administration and parents approved. It was official. I had won teacher of the year in 2004, which included an engraved crystal award as well as a $1000 check. It was undeniable affirmation and totally a gift from God.

Honestly, I don't feel like I deserved that award. I do know that I was doing a good job and had made great strides in the classroom for a new teacher. I don't, however, feel like I was the best teacher at the school. God granted this award to me. The only reason I could come up with is that He was pleased with the changes I made in my life and wanted a concrete way to let me know it. I can't overlook the fact that in awarding me the honor, God was also preparing me to say yes to the other plans He had for me. It wasn't long after that I was presented with working as a part of the Encounter Program and offered the Director of Admissions position in addition to teaching. There was no more concrete way to let me know that I was supposed to be a teacher than for me to receive the most prestigious teaching award the school offered. Even though He didn't have to, God granted me that award.

As for my decision to move back to Florida, the rewards were endless. I had never felt so secure in my relationships with both family and friends. I had started out living with my parents and even after I moved out I would still see them every week. My sister and I became close friends again and we always included each other in our plans. I strengthened my relationship with my childhood buddy, Miguel, whom I have known for 20 years. And of course I was able to be a part of the following family milestones in those first two years that I moved back to Florida: parents' 30th anniversary, grandparents' 50th anniversary, grandfather's 75th birthday, mother's 50th birthday, father's 60th birthday, great-grandmother's last days on this earth. It was entirely obvious to me that I would have missed most of those events had I not followed God's call for my life.

The best and most obvious signs of affirmation in my life were still yet to come. They involved the meeting, courtship, and marriage to my wife. The entire experience of our wedding was strewn with signs of affirmation that could only come from God. He used this most blessed of experiences to give us a message and to show His faithfulness. Chills run down my spine when I think about God's hand in Susan's and my wedding. I'm not talking about the fact that it was the happiest day of my life. Things happened on the days leading up to and the days following the wedding that can only be explained as divine intervention.

We were bursting with anticipation in the days leading up to the big event. Our wedding was destined to be perfect. The ceremony would be held at the church that my deceased grandparents, George and Angele Sayour, founded. Our families were integrally involved in very special ways. My mom helped with everything from invitations to centerpieces. Susan's stepmother would make the cake and giveaways. Both of our fathers provided for us with their generosity. My grandfather secretly planned to pray over us at the reception and my grandmother conspired to be the Master of Ceremonies for the event. We even asked two of my uncles to take pictures and video. Family and friends would fly in from places like California, New York, Connecticut, Delaware, Maine, and Georgia. It was staggering to think about all of the things that would happen and all of the people we would see on that day.

I went through my normal morning routine on the day of my wedding. I spent my last moments as a single man in a ritualistic series of events that concluded with me tightening the bow tie around my neck. My life from there on out would be shared entirely with another person. I was fully aware of that fact. I never had cold feet about it but there were mild apprehensions about whether or not I'd be a good husband and if I really deserved someone as magnificent as Susan. There were definitely aspects of my personal life of which I wasn't proud. I knew I was already forgiven for these flaws but still I couldn't help but feel like Susan deserved better.

Just before I left the hotel room I took a moment and prayed. I prayed with all my heart. I then picked up the Bible and asked God to speak directly to Susan and me. I wanted a message for our lives. I couldn't have been more amazed with the Lord's response. I ended up in the book of Jeremiah. In the thirty-third chapter and third verse I read: "Call to me and I will answer you and tell you great and unsearchable things you do not know. For this is what the Lord, God of Israel, says…"

I just instinctively skipped without knowing what followed and ended up at verse six, which reads: "Nevertheless, I will bring health and healing to it; I will heal my people and will let them enjoy abundant peace and security." Once again I moved on and came upon verse 8: "I will cleanse them from all the sin they have committed against me and will forgive all their sins of rebellion against me. Then this city (*marriage*) will bring me renown, joy, praise and honor before all nations on earth that hear of all the good things I do for it; and they will be in awe and tremble at the abundant prosperity and peace I provide for it."

Somehow the Holy Spirit pointed out the verses that I was to read. It was as if they were highlighted. The message was handpicked for Susan and me and ever so applicable. It was my concern that I was not worthy of this wonderful woman God was giving me. This Scripture clearly pointed out that, yes, there was sin and rebellion but God was past that. With this sacramental covenant I was about to make, all of those sins would be wiped away. I had come to God with all my heart and He knew it. Without letting me waste even another second on worry or concern He pointed me to the perfect place in His Word.

Once again, God didn't have to do this. I already knew that I was doing the right thing. It wasn't as if I was unsure about marrying Susan. But He knew this word was what I needed to hear and He granted it to me. What further astonishes me about this Scripture is that it not only speaks about God wiping the slate clean; it also speaks about bringing glory to God. At the very moment when I was reading the verse I instantly understood that my marriage to Susan would bring glory to God. It would bring Him "renown, joy, praise and honor before all nations on earth." Not only would God not be ashamed of my sin but my life would actually bring glory to God. What an awesome responsibility.

Did you happen to notice the last part of that verse? It reads, "…all nations on earth that hear of all the good things I do for it; and they will be in awe and tremble at the abundant prosperity and peace I provide for it." God reaffirmed the promise He had made to me in Jeremiah 29. He was extending that prophecy of hope and prosperity to my marriage.

All of this I received in a matter of seconds. It was all made clear to me and the meaning was as obvious as the light of day. I realize that the skeptics reading this book are saying I completely tailored that Scripture to meet my circumstances—and that may be so. But I maintain that God directed me to that page in the Bible and placed my eyes perfectly on those verses. Within a matter of seconds I clearly understood the message I was being given. There was no coincidence. My heart was open and God spoke.

Perhaps the best part about the whole experience was that God told me to share it with Susan. So on the first night of our honeymoon I opened the Bible and read the passage to Susan. Her eyes welled with tears. Something very powerful was released deep inside of her. The Scripture not only applied to how I was feeling; it completely applied to her. She, too, was harboring feelings that she wished would leave her. I could see in her eyes that she had gotten God's message loud and clear. Her sins were forgiven. The wedding was a new beginning. Our lives would bring glory to God. God's promise of prosperity in Jeremiah 29 was reiterated in Jeremiah 33 and our lives would forever be blessed.

Another really cool thing happened on the day of the wedding. Actually it wasn't so cool at the time but God used it for His glory in a way that only God could do. The deejay didn't show up. I remember it as if it were yesterday. I realized it immediately. Susan and I took some pictures on the Miami waterfront and I tried to keep it to myself. Finally as we were about to make our entrance to the reception I broke the news to her. I said, "Can you handle disappointment?" To which she responded, "What happened?" I replied, "The deejay didn't show up." I couldn't believe my ears when Susan said ever so sweetly, "That's all right." She wasn't going to allow anything to ruin that day.

It's really amazing. Susan and I planned the whole wedding together. Our parents had helped us out very generously with their time and with their wallets. Still though, we were on a shoestring budget and there were some questions about whether or not things would run smoothly. The one detail in which we were confident was the deejay. He was extremely professional and we felt completely secure that he would own up to his end of the deal. Well, he didn't. But this is where God came in.

We didn't have our wedding song because the deejay had assured us he would bring all the music. The only thing we could muster up as a substitute was an instrumental CD that my cousin had in her car. Susan and I ended up dancing to an instrumental version of the song "Endless Love." It was actually very romantic and I hadn't heard the song in years. Here's where it gets good.

We left that night for our honeymoon in the Jamaican city of Ocho Rios. It was a nightmarish trip. We were already exhausted from the day's events. My best man and his fiancé drove us to the airport. It took us forever to get on our way and then we drove up on two different accidents and subsequent traffic jams. I was completely relieved to finally get checked in for the flight. As we were going through security, the guard stopped me. He told me to take "it" out of my bag. Of course I didn't know what he was talking about. He said that he'd find it himself. Security then reached into my backpack and pulled out my Swiss Army knife. He was definitely perturbed but he told me I could go back and check it in. There was no way I was going back through all the lines and risk missing my flight. I ended up having to relinquish the knife and watch it get tossed in the disposables bin with the nail clippers and cigarette lighters.

This ridiculous mishap has seemingly benign significance to the story I know. But what you don't know is that I loved that knife. It was a gift from my Uncle George when I was in the 8th grade. It was the only possession I had from my childhood that I still used all the time. I took it on all my fishing, camping, and hiking trips. I always traveled with that knife. I couldn't believe I forgot to put it in the luggage that I was checking. That childhood gadget was a symbol of my independence. It was taken from me on the very same day that I gave up my selfish ways in order to build a life with Susan. This was God's way of telling me that there are certain parts of my life I will have to give up now but they will be well worth it.

Let's get back to "Endless Love." After the three-hour flight and a four-hour cab ride on a one-lane country road from Montego Bay to Ocho Rios we finally arrived and checked into our room. It was after 1 am. As we unpacked our bags I turned the radio on. Guess what song was on the radio. You got it—"Endless Love." Coincidence, I think not. For our entire stay in Jamaica we listened to that same radio station and didn't hear that song again. Then as we packed up our room to check out, I went to shut off the radio. Just as I attempted to do this wouldn't you know the song "Endless Love" played yet again.

God didn't need to give us these signs. He didn't need to speak to us that way. The love that we felt was real. We knew we were following His will for us. Yet God wanted to let us know that He was there with us. He wanted to let us know that He was a part of our lives and with us all along. He wanted to give us signs that we can take into the future. As times get tough and as disagreements arise we can always look back at God's involvement in our marriage. We will remember that He ordained it and that nothing can break it. And maybe He just wanted to let us know that we would have "Endless Love."

I find great joy in the fact that God has been involved in these moments with Susan and me. Whenever I have any doubts about the role God plays in our lives I think back to November 20, 2004. I remember the signs I just wrote about and the host of others that I didn't. I know God has given me ample proof that He has plans for me. I know, without a shadow of a doubt, that He has affirmed the role I have played in achieving those very plans. I am very excited for what lies ahead for Susan and me as we uncover His further will for our lives.

Chapter 10

GOD ISN'T FINISHED
WITH ME YET—
GOD'S TIMING

"Being confident of this, that he who began a good work in you
will carry it on to completion until the day of Christ Jesus"
—Philippians 1:6

Have you ever watched a person learning how to surf? I taught myself a few years back and let me tell you it isn't easy. You spend most of your time trying to paddle through the waves. All your energy is spent fighting against the current only to get thrown back toward the shore in one powerful swoop of the ocean. So you try to time it and paddle out through the break but you always seem to get pushed back to where you started. It's actually quite frustrating.

I had learned to surf in Florida but it wasn't until I spent one summer in California that I got to experience these types of waves. I could see surfers out past the break. They were sitting on their boards. Some of them were talking. Others were paddling around trying to get into position. I just couldn't understand why it was such a struggle to get out there. I knew all about duck diving, as it is called. A wave would come and I would plunge myself and the board under it only to get carried back toward the shore. This went on for what seemed like an hour. At last there was a pause between sets of waves and I was able to get out to where everyone was hanging out. It was a lot of work but I was finally in position. Now all I would have to do was catch a wave.

Catching a wave presents all kinds of other problems. Of course there's the whole issue of timing the wave just right. Then you need to stand up and balance on the board. If you can accomplish both of those feats you will then be faced with trying to navigate across and down the face of the wave so that it doesn't break on top of you. And finally, you need to be able to get off in the just the right place thus enabling you to paddle back out. All of that was obvious to me. What I wasn't prepared for was the jockeying that I would need to do just trying to gain rights to a wave. Surfers are very territorial that way.

Time and again I would have to pass up a wave because someone would get on it first or cut me off to get to it. I was right there but I couldn't seem to succeed at even attempting to catch a wave. Every now and again I would get my shot and then I'd usually fall right off the board. It was an extremely humbling, and not to mention exhausting, experience.

All of that would be forgotten though as I caught my first wave. I still remember the feeling. I spotted the wave while it was just a swell way out on the horizon. As it neared it began to build. I felt as if I were in a zone and the wave was coming right for me. As I began to paddle, the wave seemed to lift me up off the surface of the water. Then at just the right time I stopped paddling and popped up on the board. I was riding the wave. What a feeling! For anyone who has never experienced riding a wave you feel weightless as you glide across and then down the face. The ride, while only a few seconds long, seemed to last forever. Then just as quickly as it began it was over again. I would have to paddle back out through the break, jockey for position in the crowd, find my zone with a certain wave, and ride it all the way to completion. I would do all of that just to regain the feeling that lasts for only a few seconds.

You may be wondering what this story has to do with this book. The saga of a surfer paddling through the ocean to catch a wave provides an uncanny analogy for the plans that God has for us. Let's analyze what the surfer goes through on his or her journey to ride the perfect wave. As a side note, I'm going to use feminine pronouns so as not to offend any of the female surfers out there. Many a day I've been in the ocean and was put to shame by a member of the opposite sex.

First the surfer must really want it. The surfer knows that riding a wave for even only a few seconds is well worth the process it takes to get to that point. The surfer must persevere. She must paddle out through adverse conditions knowing that at any moment a wave can come and knock her back to where she began. Yet she forges on. Then once the obstacles are overcome and the surfer is past the break she must wait. There are different aspects to the waiting. First she must wait for a wave or a set of waves to come rolling in. Then the surfer will need to wait for her turn. And when it is finally her turn and she attempts to ride the waves she must bravely paddle in and stand up on the board. Once the whole experience is complete the surfer will go through it all again to capture the feeling she gets from what amounts to just a few seconds on a wave.

Like a wave, God's plans take time to develop. Some waves come from halfway around the globe before they finally break on a coastline. God's plans have been put into motion from the beginning of time. So what seems like a long time for us is actually a relatively short time to God. How often in our lives are we waiting for the perfect wave? We sit up attentively and wait. Yet it doesn't come. We trust in God and know that His plans will happen for us but the waiting practically kills us.

God's timing is a funny thing. Consider the story of Mary, Martha, and Lazarus. These were friends of Jesus. They appear in the Gospels many times. John 11:5 says: "Jesus loved Martha and her sister and Lazarus." Lazarus became sick while Jesus was away. In verse 6 we read: "Yet when he heard Lazarus was sick, he stayed where he was two more days." So here you have Jesus' close friends whom He often stayed with while in Bethany and they have a problem. This is not just any problem but the kind of problem that ends in death. What does Jesus choose to do? He decides to wait two days before going to His friends.

Of course we all know the story. Right? Jesus goes back to Judea and raises Lazarus from the dead. But the question remains: Why did Jesus wait two days? Why didn't He just cure Lazarus the way that He cured the centurion's servant? He could have thought it and it would have been done. We find the answer to this question in verse 4 of the same chapter. Jesus says, "This sickness will not end in death. No, it is for God's glory so that God's Son may be glorified." Jesus waited two days on purpose for two reasons. First and foremost He waited so that He could fulfill His Father's plan. Secondly, He waited to test the faith of Mary and Martha, for in verses 25-26 we read: "I am the resurrection and the life. He who believes in me will live, even though he dies; and whoever lives and believes in me will never die. Do you believe this?" Martha replied yes and Lazarus was raised from the dead.

Consider the prophet Daniel. He was so concerned about his circumstances that he mourned, fasted, and prayed for three weeks. When the three weeks were up an angel appeared to him and said in Daniel 10, verse 12: "Do not be afraid, Daniel. Since the first day that you set your mind to gain understanding and to humble yourself before God, your words were heard, and I have come in response to them." Think about that for a moment. The angel acknowledged that Daniel's prayers from three weeks prior were heard. Yet it took three weeks for the angel to come to Daniel. God's timing is definitely a funny thing.

The lesson in this is persistence. Just like the surfer paddling through the waves, Daniel forged on. He prayed and prayed for three weeks with faith that his prayers would break through. Martha requested that Jesus come and heal her brother. Jesus waited two days. When He arrived, Martha acknowledged that Jesus could have saved Lazarus. She then followed it up with: "But I know that even now God will give you whatever you ask" (John 11:22). Both Martha and Daniel had faith. Even though their prayers weren't answered on their timing they remained persistent. They persevered through the setbacks just as the surfer perseveres through the barrage of waves. And both came out victoriously on the other side.

In my own life I have an example of a prayer that God chose to answer eight months later. The funny thing is that I didn't realize it until twelve years after that. I had just turned 17 and it was my junior year of high school. I was actually on the four-day Encounter retreat as a student and I remember praying.

I was at a point in my life when I had begun driving and I was approaching my senior year of high school. I prayed that God would introduce me to a girl whom I could become close to and date. I really wanted someone with whom to share things. A year and a half later I graduated from high school and the prayer was left unanswered. Or so I thought.

I only recently realized that I was introduced to Susan, my wife, shortly after that prayer. Susan and I first met in a course called Honors English 4 in August of our senior year. Of course at that time I didn't know she was God's answer to my request. Had that meeting not taken place in high school I never would have reunited with her in Fort Lauderdale a whole decade later. It was on an Encounter retreat as an adult leader when I realized that Susan was the answer to the prayer I had said in that very same building twelve years earlier. God chose to fulfill my prayer and to do it on His timing. In high school I met the girl I would marry even though it took twelve years to be fulfilled. It would have been easy for Susan and me to let our meeting pass us by like a wave in the ocean. We instead realized the sign that God was giving us and both decided to paddle into the relationship. I'm sure glad we did.

God's plans for us are very much like a wave in the ocean. They often start as a result of a ripple that occurs off in the distance. Even though we are unaware, the plans are in motion. Then the wave draws closer. It begins to take shape and the final form becomes eminent. It is at this time that the surfer has a choice to make. He can decide to paddle in or to let the wave go by him. He must have faith that he can surf the wave and that it will be worth it. In the same way God's plans begin to take shape. We can see them coming and we will have a decision to make. We must have faith that this is God's path for us and that we can accomplish His will. And once we finish riding the wave or completing the task God is asking us to do, we must paddle back out in an effort to ride yet another wave and continue to do the work the Lord has for us.

God's plans for us are a process. They are set into motion well in advance of our existence. The plans are never merely fulfilled. They will continue with us until we unite with our Creator and Father in heaven. While on this earth we will have a series of stops on our journey and a number of waves to surf. Each one will require a surfer-like process. We will need to overcome obstacles, have patience for God's timing, and then choose to act. Each one will offer us an opportunity to fulfill God's plans for our lives. In the end we will be able to look back on our lives and connect the dots of the different waves we have surfed while recounting the decisions and instances that each dot represents.

As I look at my own journey I am amazed at how well the pieces of the puzzle of my life fit together. My story begins before I was even born. Both sets of my grandparents were of Syrian descent. Both of my grandfathers' were named George. It was only natural then for my parents to name me after their fathers. I grew up in a very traditional home where hard work was celebrated. I had a lot to live up to since both sides of my family came to the U.S. in the early 1900s with nothing and made successful and comfortable lives for themselves.

Through the examples of my parents I put God first, family next, and education third. With this formula I excelled in my relationships and in my schoolwork. Due to our gifted abilities, my sister and I transferred to a better grade school than the one that we were attending. When it was time to choose high schools I had a really tough decision to make. Out of the 70 students in my 8th grade class, 60 of them had applied to one particular school. I really felt led toward another school and was forced to leave my main group of friends at the time. Luckily my very best friend decided on the same high school. Not too long after, I learned that I would be reunited with my cousins due to this decision.

In high school I got involved on the cross-country and track teams. These experiences instilled in me a healthy lifestyle and gave me the lifelong friendships of my coach and teammates. During my junior year I went on my first Encounter retreat and prayed for God to put someone in my life. The next year I met Susan. I still remember being distracted by her in English class and as she was rollerblading on the beach while I was playing volleyball. During this time in my life I watched my Uncle Paul graduate from college and become a Mechanical Engineer with General Electric. I had always looked up to him and decided to follow in his footsteps. It was at this time that God directed me to go to RPI instead of Georgia Tech and He provided me with the means to do so.

Going away to school forced me to become self-sufficient and responsible. I became my own man. During this time I solidified my love for nature, the outdoors, and travel. I regularly participated in hobbies such as whitewater kayaking, mountain biking, camping, fishing, hiking, and in-line skating. It was during my junior year that I decided I should get some hands-on experience. I found out about a research project that was looking for an assistant. The project involved plastic injection molding. The summer after my junior year I decided to take part in RPI's

Co-op program for eight months. I accepted a job working as a mechanical engineer in a plastic injection molding company just outside of Albany, NY, called Southco, Inc. I was blessed enough to have an aunt and uncle nearby who generously let me live with them during this time.

While working for Southco, I obtained some much-needed confidence. I learned that I could make it in industry. I figured out how companies operated and how employees should function within them. The most invaluable lesson that I learned during this job was to listen to people. I spent countless hours working with and learning from the maintenance crew of the facility. They had so much knowledge and experience and yet they were often overlooked. I was blessed that at the end of that eight-month assignment my manager asked me to stay on. I worked for Southco for almost two years while I went to college. The money I earned helped me to lessen the burden on my parents who were dealing with issues of having to relocate their business at the time.

It was because I worked at Southco that I was able to land the job with Procter & Gamble. While at Procter & Gamble I developed lifelong friends, traveled the world, and gained much responsibility and experience. Perhaps one of the greatest tools that I obtained from my P&G days is the ability to speak in front of people. Within the first few months of working at P&G, my bosses indicated that I would need to work on my presentation techniques. I was scared to death of public speaking but I was in a sink-or-swim situation so I worked on it. Four years later that weakness was actually hailed as a strength. Even in my last month with the company my manager had me present to a few directors that came to tour the plant.

At this point you know what follows next. I left Procter & Gamble, moved home, and started teaching. Within a relatively short period of time I was named Teacher of the Year, was made the Director of Admissions, and was co-leading retreats. I never would have gotten that award or promotions had I not worked at Procter & Gamble where I learned my organizational and public speaking skills. It was also at this time where my life came full circle. I was teaching at the school that I attended, coaching a team that I was a member of, co-leading a retreat that I was a participant in, and dating a girl that I had been friends with.

My entire life has been a process of God's plans that have taken time to fulfill. If even one of the stages of my life had happened differently I would not be where I am today. If my parents and grandparents hadn't instilled in me godly priorities, then I would not have put God first, family second, and education third. I wouldn't have excelled in my course work. This could have jeopardized the opportunities I had in the grade schools and high schools I attended. If I went to a different high school I would not have joined the cross-country team, I wouldn't have gone on Encounter, and I never would have met Susan. Therefore I wouldn't have an affinity towards healthy living; I wouldn't be teaching at that high school; I wouldn't be leading retreats, and I certainly wouldn't have married Susan. If my uncle had not been a mechanical engineer, I wouldn't have thought of pursuing a career as one also. If I didn't go to RPI who knows what job I'd be holding today. While at RPI if I hadn't volunteered for the plastic injection molding research project, I would not have gotten the Co-op assignment with Southco, the plastic injection molding company. Southco gave me the experience that P&G was looking for and was probably the reason they overlooked the GPA requirement. P&G taught me the organizational, analytical, and public speaking skills that I would need to be successful as a teacher, retreat director, and Director of Admissions.

Through all of this I am convinced that God is not finished with me yet. In Jeremiah 29, we see that God knows what we've been through, wants to prosper us now in our current situation, and has amazing future plans for us. I know there is so much more He has for me and I look forward to adding to the connected dots of my life. In His own time, God will complete in me the work and plan that only He knows for my life.

At this point I'd ask you to reread the Scripture with which I opened this chapter. Think about it and answer the following questions about your own life. "Being confident of this, that he who began a good work in you will carry it on to completion until the day of Christ Jesus" (Philippians 1:6).

What are the different waves you have surfed in your own life? What obstacles did you have to overcome to ride them? What prayers did God take awhile to answer, but when He did you realized they were worth the wait? How was one situation you were in used as a building block for the next situation you would face? What are the dots in your life that connect your birth to where you stand as a person right now?

Part 3

PRACTICAL STEPS IN APPLYING JEREMIAH 29 TO YOUR OWN LIFE

"For I know the plans I have for you," declares the Lord, "plans to prosper you and not to harm you, plans to give you hope and a future. Then you will call upon me and come and pray to me, and I will listen to you. You will seek me and find me when you seek me with all your heart. I will be found by you," declares the Lord, "and will bring you back from captivity. I will gather you from all the nations and places where I have banished you," declares the Lord, "and bring you back to the place from which I carried you into exile."

—Jeremiah 29:11-14

Chapter 11

IT'S A MATTER OF THE HEART

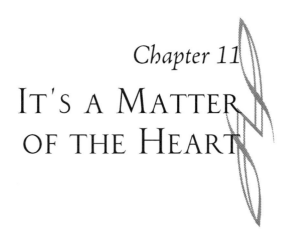

"You will seek me and find me when you seek me with all your heart"

—Jeremiah 29:13

What does it mean to seek God with all our hearts? For most people this concept is extremely hard to grasp. I have been a believer in God and in Jesus for as long as I have been able to speak. It wasn't until recently that I realized I am just beginning to understand what it means to seek God with all of my heart. For many people this is a hard distinction to make. Believing in God is an entirely different thing from seeking God, having faith in God, and even loving God.

The word *heart* or some alternative for *heart* appears throughout the King James Bible almost 1000 times. The topic of the heart is one of the most central concepts of the entire Bible. It is one of the unifying themes between the Old Testament and the New Testament. The message just doesn't change. As we have already seen in Jeremiah 29:13 God says to His people: "You will seek me and find me when you seek me with all your heart." In Matthew 22:37, Jesus tells us that the greatest commandment is to, "Love the Lord your God with all your heart and with all your soul and with all your mind." Through thousands of years of Scripture nothing has changed. We are to seek God and we are to love God with all our hearts.

To believe that there is a God is an entirely different concept from having faith in God. Our society just doesn't get this point. We have become a culture of people who believe there is a God or don't believe there is a God. But that really isn't the question. The question is: Do you have faith in God? There is no risk at all in merely believing that God exists. Actually it takes the same amount of effort to believe that there is a God and to be an atheist. It comes down to a choice. Atheists would have you believe that it is naïve to think God exists. Monotheists will take the stance that God must exist because it is impossible to get something out of nothing and therefore the creation of the universe must have begun due to a supernatural force. In either case the person is required to make a choice and that is all.

This wasn't always the case, though. There was once a time when it was taken for granted that God did indeed exist. So the question wasn't whether or not a person believed in God; it was taken for granted that there was a god or gods. All throughout the Old Testament the enemies of the Israelites acknowledged that the God of Israel existed. There is a clear illustration of this in 1 Samuel, chapters 5 and 6. The Philistines had captured the ark of the Lord from the Jews and all kinds of evil befell them. The Philistines themselves worshipped their god known as Dagon. Here is what they discussed amongst themselves: "What shall we do with the ark of the Lord? Tell us how we should send it back to its place" (1 Samuel 6:2). Notice that they didn't say, "What shall we do with this ark of the Jews." They said "ark of the Lord." The Philistines obviously recognized the power of the God of Israel yet they chose not to serve Him.

So the question still remains: How do we transition from belief in God and even in Jesus to having faith in God and seeking God with all our hearts? Many people believe that this requires a lot of work. They think we must spend hours a day praying and maybe even change our personalities. This is not the case at all. Seeking God with all our hearts is a change that takes place deep inside a person. The Apostle Paul writes in Romans 12:2: "Do not conform any longer to the pattern of this world, but be transformed by the renewing of your mind. Then you will be able to test and approve what God's will is—His good, pleasing, and perfect will." The change takes place inside first. We must renew our minds.

The feeling of the need to be transformed originates in the heart. Your heart tells your mind that your soul needs to change direction. Your mind can then choose what to do with this information. It may decide to ignore the feeling. Your mind may even decide to rationalize the feeling away. As you delay the decision more and more discontent will enter your life. Once your mind accepts and stops fighting the message that your heart is sending, you are ready to make the change. But until your mind stops fighting the feeling you will be unable to act on it. Once the choice is made you can begin to live out that choice. This is only the beginning of the process.

In my own life it was obvious that my heart was sending my mind the message that I was missing something. I didn't want to acknowledge that God was missing from my life. I was trying to have the best of both worlds. I believed that there was a God and even claimed to be a follower of Christ but my actions were no witness to these claims. I was living for myself and even if my mind was convinced of the pureness of my behavior there was no fooling my heart. The longer I delayed coming to grips with the messages that the Holy Spirit was sending to me the unhappier I became with life. It was on the trip to Florida when my mind became transformed and I no longer sought the ways of the world.

By leaving Procter & Gamble for a better life, I definitely broke the hold that the pattern of the world had on my life. I then began to pursue God's will for me. But it didn't end there. Had it ended there I'm sure there would have been another wake-up call. God was patient with me once the wheels were in motion. He led me in the direction He wanted me to go. He strategically placed people and experiences in my life that would direct me on the path that would fulfill His will. Then He affirmed my decisions just to let me know that I was on the right track. I showed evidence of all this in the previous chapters. All of these events were leading up to the next part of my spiritual journey.

It was after the series of affirmations in my life that God had a little talk with me. In essence here is what He said. "All right, George. You've acknowledged that I am God and you've sought to do My will but there is still something missing. You're really good at going through the doors that I open for you. You're getting better at going down the right path. But I want more. I expect more. You're a good listener but you're just not sharing. Talk to me, George. Really share with me." I used to share with God. I used to talk with God all day long—while in the car, when I was kayaking on the river—but somewhere along the way I turned to solely listening. I had to put both parts together to take the next step on my spiritual journey with the Lord.

Once the channels of communication were reopened between God's heart and my own I began to feel differently about my life and what I was doing. I began to seek God's will over my own. Before I was looking for God's will to coincide with my own. I knew I was unhappy at Procter & Gamble and so I looked to make a change that would follow God's plan for me as long as I approved of it. But that was starting to change inside of me. I began to understand what the sovereignty of God meant. The sovereignty of God means that since He created this world and everything in it, then He is in control. Not only is He in control but His will supercedes everyone else's. That means that we won't always agree with what He does. We, in turn, must accept His will because He is God.

Therefore, once you believe in God there are three things that must happen in order for you to say you are seeking Him with all your heart. First, you must listen to God. Where is He leading you? What is He telling you to do? Follow His direction. Go through the doors that He opens in your life. Second, you must talk to God. Tell Him how much you love Him. Give Him the attention that you want from Him. Ask Him for His will for your life. What comes of those two-way conversations will be the key to this whole experience and the third action that must take place. You must turn your life over to God, accept that He is sovereign, and follow His will for you even if it is not your own and was not a part of your plan.

In my own life I became a teacher not only for the impact that I would have on the students but also because I felt that being a teacher would allow me the type of life I wanted to live.

I wanted time off. I wanted to get out of project work with deadlines. I wanted to leave the rat race behind. God granted that. But this achievement was just a part of the positioning process that God was using to ready me for the next step. As I truly began to communicate with God I realized there was more that He wanted me to do. I accepted this.

There were three things God wanted me to do at that point. First God wanted me to be a part of the Encounter retreat program at the school. This would require many extra hours and much responsibility. Next God wanted me to be the Director of Admissions of the school. This assignment would require project work, putting on events, and certainly deadlines. Third and most importantly, God wanted me to marry Susan.

My relationship with Susan would be the most difficult hurdle. I certainly loved her. Love wasn't the issue. I just wasn't sure if marriage was for me. But through the seeking of God with all my heart He told me to give it a chance. So I did. And boy, am I glad I did. I thought that I loved Susan before I came to that realization. That love was just a fraction of what I felt toward her after I got that message from God. His message to me freed up capacities for giving and receiving love that I didn't know I had. And our relationship has been growing since.

Funny things happen when we seek God. Our whole world begins to change. We start to see things differently. Instead of trying to figure out what we should do for ourselves we ask how we can best fulfill God's will. Selfishness leaves our lives altogether. Our own accomplishments are recognized to be His. And most importantly we achieve a peace that words cannot describe.

In order to get to this state we must totally and without reservation turn our lives over to God. I have the perfect example of what I'm talking about—something that is going on in my life right now. Susan and I, like most married couples, are a two-income family out of necessity. Susan is aspiring to pursue a career change that would require us to do without her income for at least three months. We had been putting this off for about a year since we didn't know where the money would come from to pay the bills. At about this same time we began to become more generous with our charitable giving. God, in turn, blessed us with some investment opportunities that would provide us with the income that we needed to get by in the interim for when Susan would not be working.

As you read this story it would be easy to assume that the hook is God provided the means for us to support ourselves since we have been seeking Him with all our hearts. Well that's what I thought as well. Then just three weeks ago, something happened. One of the investments went bad. I had already used much of the profits I had received and this loss set us back substantially—not exactly the ending you were expecting, now was it? Well, here's my take on it. As the money came in, I began to trust in it. I became secure that we had figured out a way for Susan to quit her job and pursue her dreams. This is not what God wants at all. He does not want us to rely on our successes and accomplishments. Jesus wants us to trust in Him.

The disappointment on Susan's face as I told her the news was almost unbearable. She feared that she would have to stay in her current less-than-ideal work situation. I felt as if I had let her down and her disappointment was hard to take. As we dealt with the blow of the loss of money I asked her if she felt led to make this career change, to which she replied yes. I, of course, knew the answer but I wanted to hear it from her. I then discussed with her that we would continue as planned with her leaving her job at the end of the next month. I told her how silly it would be for us to feel comfortable making the move based on our efforts, but uneasy about it when we had to trust in God. God has never failed us and He won't now.

I feel that God is using this current situation to show us that He will take care of us. He also wants to test us a little. It's easy to trust in God when things are running smoothly. Real faith sets in when times are uncertain. I don't know what the outcome of this situation will be. I do know that God is going to be there with us every step of the way. As Jesus said in Luke 12:22-24: "Therefore I tell you, do not worry about your life, what you will eat; or about your body, what you will wear. Life is more than food, and the body more than clothes. Consider the ravens: They do not sow or reap, they have no storeroom or barn; yet God feeds them. And how much more valuable you are than birds!"

God wants us to know that our successes and conquests are actually His successes and conquests. Had the investment not gone bad I could have concluded that I provided for the family and that I made the money. I could have reveled in the idea that I enabled those things and therefore Susan would be able to pursue her dreams. By God allowing the financial losses in my life I am now forced to trust in God. The test then becomes: Do we go ahead and follow through with God's plan for Susan or do we hold off for fear that we will not be able to provide for our needs? The answer that we have chosen is to forge ahead and go where God is leading us despite the fact that we are not financially ready for that endeavor. We have given this situation to God.

Seeking God with all your heart is a process. You know that you are doing it if you are talking to God, listening to God, and turning your life and all that you encounter over to Him. This process does not happen by itself. It takes time and commitment just as any relationship does. In other words, just because you make the choice that you are going to love God and seek Him with all your heart doesn't mean that it will come naturally or automatically. You need to exercise your spiritual muscles in order to achieve this. The more you talk to God, listen to God, and put God first, the easier it will get.

Consider a scenario in which you want to run a marathon. The mere decision to have this goal doesn't make you achieve it. You would need to train and practice. If you went out and attempted to run the whole thing at once you'd undoubtedly fail. Instead, you would work up to it. You would go for jogs and see how your body reacts. Each day, perhaps, you'd go a little farther. You would have to refrain from putting into your body certain things like alcohol, cigarettes, soda, and fast foods. You would need to make sure that you ate the right foods, drank the right fluids, and got enough rest. The more seriously you took it, the more comfortable and natural that it would feel. It would get to the point where you could easily go out and run five or even ten miles without thinking about it. You would see the progress and understand how you could achieve your goal of completing a marathon. Through all of this you will be building your physical muscles and cardiovascular system. They would develop to be able to perform in the environment in which you are demanding them to operate.

Our relationship with God is similar to the goal of running a marathon. Just deciding to have a relationship with God doesn't mean that you will have one. It will take practice. The more you try to love God the easier it will get and the more natural it will feel. You will have to be sure to purge from your life certain aspects that impede your progress of getting to know God. In addition you will need to make sure to include in your life things and people that will strengthen your ability to achieve your goal of loving God. All the while your spiritual muscles will be growing to fit the environment in which you are demanding them to operate.

Let's summarize. We know that in order to seek God and love God with all our hearts we must do at least three things. First, we must listen to God. What is God asking me to do? In what direction is the Holy Spirit telling me to go? Secondly, we must talk to God. What do I want to tell Jesus? What do I want to ask God? And finally, we must turn our lives over to God. Where do I put my trust? What in my life comes before God? If we do these three things and address the questions that follow we will be on the path to seeking and loving God with all our hearts.

Chapter 12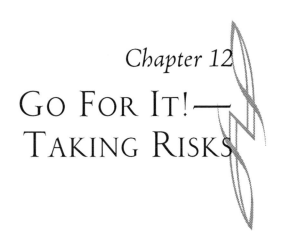

GO FOR IT!—
TAKING RISKS

"I can do all things through Christ who strengthens me"
—Philippians 4:13 NKJV

A boy named David stood up against a giant called Goliath. A girl named Esther defied royal orders in order to save her people. A man named Noah built an ark on dry ground. A teenage girl named Mary said yes to be the mother of God. A prophet named Elijah stood up for the Lord against 450 of Baal's prophets. A Pharisee named Saul stopped persecuting the followers of Christ and became an apostle himself. The Son of God named Jesus obeyed His Father's will and laid down His life for us. All of these individuals defied conventional wisdom and cultural norms to follow God's will for their lives. They all knew one key tenet of life. "If God is for us, who can be against us?" (Romans 8:31).

We have such good examples of people fulfilling God's purpose for their lives, yet we struggle so much with this in our own.

Often we know what we are supposed to do. We even know that God wants us to do it. But, due to fear, we don't follow through or even attempt to accomplish the task. We become afraid of the effect the outcome will have on our lives. We ask ourselves questions: What will my friends think? What will my family think? What will my coworkers think? How can I afford to do this? What if I fail? What if people laugh at me? How will this affect my plans? What if people won't like me anymore?

Or we ponder negative thoughts: But this doesn't fit with my plan. God can't want me to give that up. People will never understand. I might fail. The obstacles are too great. We worry about the cost and are afraid of failure.

We as Christians have missed a key principle of our faith: God's plans cannot fail. They must succeed. The only way we can fail is when we fail to act. Frequently the scenario goes like this. We feel that God wants us to do something. We consider all that can go wrong with the plan. We deliberate. We put it off. We may even pray. All too often, though, we refuse to act for fear of failure. In essence, we are so afraid to fail that we end up failing. Had we acted, we would most certainly have succeeded since it was God's will.

Another problem in all this is that we try to read into what God is asking us to do. We devise our own idea of what success looks like and then measure ourselves against the outcome that we constructed in our heads. But all God did was ask us to do something. He may not have told us what the end result would be or even the purpose. Often the purpose of God's plans does not become apparent until long after the task is complete. The true purpose of our actions may not manifest until we've already moved on to the next task God asks us to do. Just look around you. How many programs, groups, ideas, or churches have you come into contact with that are carrying out God's work without the original people who conceived of and carried out the plans? Lives are being touched by the continuing work of these institutions yet the people that said yes to getting them started may not even be aware of how far their work reached.

God's work must be carried out whether we get to see the fruits of our labor or not. After all, it is not about us. We are here to fulfill God's will and purpose and not our own. Too often, though, we get wrapped up in instant gratification and the desire for immediate results. Much of God's plans don't work that way. It begins with people laying groundwork and planting seeds. Once the foundation is laid we may be asked to move on and let others continue the work. We may never fully realize the impact of our involvement in doing God's work until we leave this earth. We still must do it.

Once again, we cannot fail if it is God's will. God is all-knowing and all-powerful. Therefore, He has thought of everything for us already. There is no need to worry about the details. God has taken care of all of them. Those doors that are closed are waiting to be supernaturally opened. Those mountains that are in the way will soon become molehills off to the side of the road. Since He has created us and already knows our limitations, God will never ask us to do something beyond our capability.

Is there anything in this chapter so far that you do not agree with? Look back through the past five or so paragraphs. See if there is even one sentence I wrote that is not true. I would venture to say that most of you agree with everything I've written in this chapter. Yet we often fall short when it comes to doing God's will.

Now, you might be thinking that you agree with everything I wrote but I've left something out. What about when you don't know if it is your own will or God's will? What do you do then? My response to that is you should *pray*. You pray humbly to God. He will speak to your heart. If you still feel led to do what you were thinking, then you *act*. Don't put it off for even another day. Begin researching and working toward that feeling. If it is not God's will for your life He will let you know and lead you in another direction. If you don't *act* you won't know.

I have thought about writing a book for a couple of years now. It was just an idea in my head. I pondered how I would go about doing it. I threw around ideas about subject matter. I even casually discussed it with my wife at the dinner table. It remained just an idea for well over two years. I really felt led to do this but I couldn't help but think of all of the reasons why I shouldn't do it. What would I write about? Who would publish me as an author? Who would buy the book? Would I have enough material? How long would it take? Where would I write it? What if I spend all that time and then fail? Am I even capable?

I finally realized it would remain just an idea unless I decided to *act*. So I did. I asked Susan if she would get her old laptop up and running with a word processing program. She gave it to me the next day. I began to brainstorm about all my experiences. I typed everything out. I really wanted to write a book about management styles. In the five years that I was with Procter & Gamble I had learned a lot. I figured that by sharing these experiences I could help those that would aspire to succeed in corporate America. There was one major problem. Five years was hardly a career's worth of knowledge. It wasn't like I was a Director, Vice President, or CEO. Who would listen to me? I put all of the questions and apprehensions aside and continued to brainstorm.

Through the process, *Plans to Prosper You* was born. If I merely intended to write a book I don't think I would have come up with this idea. By sitting down and doing it, God directed my thoughts. He basically said, "George, so you want to write a book. Do you think you came up with that idea on your own? Well, never mind that. I'm glad you got started. Now that you're serious about this let me show you the direction I want you to go. Write this book of yours for Me." I realized that I should share how God has directed my life. I wanted to let others know of the good news that I was feeling. All of a sudden this book began to take shape.

For two years I had made no progress toward fulfilling the urge to write a book. In order for things to happen I had to get serious about it. It was when I actually sat down at the computer and began to brainstorm that this project began to take shape. I came up with many great ideas but this one just jumped out at me. I would analyze and discuss the journey of my own life. I could help others achieve God's plan for their lives by telling my story. It was the only idea I came up with that I couldn't conceive of failing. Every other idea left me with more questions. *Plans to Prosper You* had no downside. The story had to be told. I came to realize that if God wanted my story told, then it would be told. He would give me the words to write. He would direct me down the path to get published. He would touch the people's lives with it that He wanted to touch. Had I not begun to act I would have never been able to follow the direction in which God was leading me.

Another example of taking a risk by acting on God's plans was my decision to leave Procter & Gamble. I had felt dissatisfied with my job for quite sometime. I tried many things to make it work for me. In the end I just grew more and more discontented. I knew many others in the same situation that felt the same way. We would always say that we could go and get a job with a lot of different companies. I finally decided to stop talking about it and start looking. I put my name in with a headhunter and she began to put the word out. I called someone that I knew at IBM and set up an interview with them. I was all prepared to go on that interview but since I was still working with P&G I ended up going on a last-minute trip to Cincinnati and had to cancel.

While on the plane to Ohio I had some time to think. What was the point in leaving one company to go to another? It wasn't like I was trying to get away from the management or my co-workers. It wasn't that there were no opportunities to advance. The work was my problem. So why would I leave P&G to go and do the same type of work at IBM? It was then that I realized I was running away from my job and, more specifically, my life. God doesn't want us to merely run away from a situation. If that's all that we are doing then we will inevitably end up in another equally miserable place. God wants us to run toward Him and the life He has for us. It was on that plane ride that He told me to look for something else.

I had been talking about leaving P&G for a long time. I just didn't know where I would go. It wasn't until I decided to *act* that I started to figure things out. By setting up an interview and talking with a headhunter I began the process. God then stepped in and said "All right, George. I'm glad to see that you are deciding to do something different with your life. That's the first step. But you're not searching in the right direction. Let me guide you. Follow me." A couple of months later I went to Florida to see my parents and realized what I should do.

Once I knew what God wanted me to do, the rest became easy. I put in for the separation package that P&G was offering and signed it without knowing how the plans would work out. I didn't need to know. I knew all the details that I needed to get started. As I already covered, God was leading me back to Florida. He told me to go into education. He didn't give me the specifics. He didn't give me a timeline. He just said, *Go*. So I went. I didn't know if my qualifications would match up. I didn't know if I could support myself until I got a teaching job. I didn't even know how long it would take. When I told the people I worked with what I was doing, I couldn't believe the support. What was more shocking, though, was the number of people that said they wished they could do the same thing. Some of these were third level managers who had been with the company for 20 years. They envied me.

You see if you feel like you want to do something, you'll never know unless you act. God will then use the events that transpire in your life to direct you where He wants you to go. There is an essential aspect to all of this. The most crucial and central thing you must do before, while, and after you *act* is *pray*. You need to be talking with God and listening to your heart. If you have submitted your life to God and relinquished control to Him you will know in your heart what you should do, what you should continue to do, and what you should stop doing.

Through this constant communication and awareness of God's control in your life you will instinctively know the direction you should take. That doesn't mean there won't be bumps along the way. Remember, God uses those bumps, obstacles, and mishaps to help you grow. What it does mean is that you will end up where God wants and plans for you to end up.

I don't know if this book will sell 100, 1,000, 10,000, or even more copies. I do know that each time I sit down to this computer I pray to God. I ask that He send the Holy Spirit to speak to me and through me. I ask that I write what He wants me to write. I want to make sure that I don't miss a single word He wants in this book. The number of copies it sells is irrelevant and I no longer worry about it. That is in God's hands.

My grandfather has a saying. (Actually, he has a lot of sayings but this one applies here.) He says, "God will do what God can do; now you need to do what you can do." The meaning is simple. We need to do what is in our power and then leave the details that we can't control up to God. It's a powerful statement especially for those doers in the world. I used to struggle with this. I know I can make things happen and if there is an obstacle in the way I want to remove it myself. Since I've given control of my life over to God I no longer think like that. I now realize that I'm human and I have limitations. But if what I'm doing is God's will, He will take care of what I can't.

I'll close this chapter with the story of Jonah. Jonah was a prophet of God, and a reluctant one at that. God clearly told him to go to Nineveh and to preach there. How do we know it was clear to Jonah? We know that Jonah understood God's will because he did the exact opposite of it. He got on a boat and tried to get as far away from Nineveh as he could. Don't we all do that sometimes? There are times in my life when I know that I'm supposed to do something. In order to get out of it I get sneaky. I go ahead and plan something else. I start doing something else so I can't do what I'm supposed to do. Well, that's what Jonah did. He knew that God wanted him in Nineveh and he didn't want to go.

But God had a plan and a reluctant and disobedient prophet wasn't going to stand in the way of it. The storms began to build and almost capsized the boat. In the end Jonah ended up in the sea where a giant fish swallowed him and swam him all the way to Nineveh. You see, God won't be denied. Jonah ended up doing God's will anyway. By fighting it he just made it worse for himself.

This story can and will play out in our own lives. If God wants something done it will get done. We can try to fight it. We can choose to ignore it. We can attempt to rationalize it away. In the end we will end up going through storms and rough seas until we do what we know must be done. The discontent we feel and the reason that we stay up at night will only go away by our deliberate and purposeful actions to follow God's plan for us. We must not lose sight of the Scripture passage that has brought us here. "For I know the plans I have for you," declares the Lord, "plans to prosper you and not to harm you" (Jeremiah 29:11). But those plans will not happen by themselves. We must do what we can do and God will do what He can do.

Chapter 13

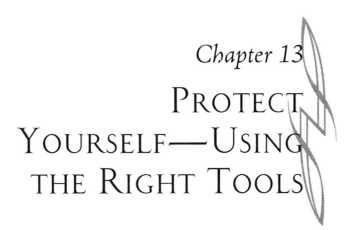

PROTECT YOURSELF—USING THE RIGHT TOOLS

"Therefore put on the full armor of God, so that when the day of evil comes, you may be able to stand your ground."
—Ephesians 6:13

J ust this past week I was camping outside of Yosemite National Park. (It was Easter Break—one of the perks of being a teacher.) My buddy, Web, and I spent our days kayaking down the Merced River. California had just been through a record bout of rain—something like 33 days in a row. Needless to say the river was swelling. Of course it was only mid-April and the other half of the water in the river was snowmelt from the mountain range that towered above.

Web and I happened to be commenting during one of the days about all the gear that was required for whitewater kayaking. We often refer to our attire as "full battle gear." Let's start from the ground up. We have neoprene booties with rubber soles on our feet. We usually wear a wet suit that covers our legs and torso. The purpose is twofold. The wet suit will, of course, keep us warm. Second, and most often overlooked, is that the wet suit offers a buffer of protection from any nicks, scrapes, bangs, and bruises should we end up upside down while going through a rapid. Then on really cold days we wear what is known as a dry top, which has rubber gaskets around the neck and wrists to keep the water out. Dry tops are a real pain to put on and take off.

The next piece of gear we sport is called a spray skirt. Spray skirts come up over our waist. The part on our torso fits inside a tunnel inside the dry top. The rim of the spray skirt fits snuggly around the cockpit of the kayak. The skirt's seal against our body and the kayak helps keep the water out of the boat, even when we are upside down. Over the wet suit, dry top, and spray skirt we wear a PFD. PFD is a fancy name for a life jacket. On our hands we wear gloves. Again, the purpose is twofold: for warmth and protection. And of course, we wear a helmet on our heads. Depending on the river the helmet may or may not have a facemask.

We have all kinds of accessories that we attach to our gear as well. In the zipper of my PFD I carry a whistle. This way if I need to alert someone up or down river I can get his or her attention. You'd be surprised how loud the things can be. Also secured to my PFD is a quick release knife just in case I end up tangled in a safety rope or caught under a raft. Don't laugh; I've ended up underneath two whitewater rafts in my life—not fun. I also carry a rope bag strapped to my waist. I can't count how many times I've used a rope to rescue a fellow kayaker or have been rescued by one myself.

Whether we go on a daylong kayaking trip or just kayak a mile or two we need most, if not all, of that gear. I would never consider going down even a class II stretch of river without a helmet or a PFD. It has been during the times when I wasn't wearing my gloves or wet suit that I needed them the most. I once knew a guy who forgot his life jacket and decided to paddle without it. Wouldn't you know that he was coming over a ledge and clipped a rock with his chest? It knocked the wind right out of him and flipped his kayak completely over. Luckily he was all right. As for me, at this point I have been kayaking rivers long enough to know better than to leave any of my safety and protective gear at home.

Much can be learned from the precautions that are involved in participating in extreme sports. Most of the gear we use while whitewater kayaking is there merely as a precaution. My helmet may not see a scratch for months. Then when I least expect it my boat goes over and my head slams square into a boulder. Believe me, on those days I'm glad I have it. At first a lifejacket can feel bulky and restricting. After awhile a person will become accustomed to the feel and not even notice it is on anymore. We go through the initial awkwardness of using these tools even though we may not need them all the time. We put them on just in case a situation may arise down the road (river) that will require their support. Over time the awkwardness wears off and it becomes second nature to use and wear these devices. They become extensions of our bodies while inside the kayak.

Many hours of practice go into being able to kayak down even a class III river. I'll bet I've spent almost as much time flipping myself over and then rolling back up on flat water as I have on real rivers. Over and over I would practice. I would rehearse doing it with my paddle in different positions. I even practiced it without a paddle. I wanted to be absolutely certain that *when* I flip over on a river in high current and big waves I will be able to roll myself back up. I stress the word *when*. I don't know anyone who kayaks who doesn't end up upside down sooner or later. It is part of the sport. Many a day on the river has been defined by whether or not a person was able to roll up in their kayak or if he or she ended up swimming down the river.

Our journey through life and walk with the Lord requires similar precautions and preparations yet somehow so many of us are unwilling to do what is necessary. Like the kayaker we go out time and again knowing that we will meet obstacles and eventually we will flip over. But unlike the kayaker we are unprepared for the situation. We are left upside down in life flailing about with no rehearsed routine or procedure to set ourselves right side up. We don't even wear our battle gear for those times in life when we will get banged around and left gasping for air. How can we ever achieve the plans God has for us if we are not prepared to meet head-on the obstacles that are in the way of those plans.

The apostle Paul said it best in Ephesians 6:13-18. Here he writes: "Therefore put on the full armor of God, so that when the day of evil comes, you may be able to stand your ground, and after you have done everything, to stand. Stand firm then, with the belt of truth buckled around your waist, with the breastplate of righteousness in place, and with your feet fitted in readiness that comes from the gospel of peace. In addition to all this, take up the shield of faith, with which you can extinguish all the flaming arrows of the evil one. Take the helmet of salvation and the sword of the Spirit, which is the word of God. And pray in the Spirit on all occasions."

He makes it sound as if we're going into battle. Paul uses the words *armor, belt, breastplate, shield,* and *helmet.* You can't help but get the feeling that he wants us to be protected. In a lot of ways we are going to battle. There are so many forces in this world that are working against us. It becomes overwhelming and we often don't know where to turn. If we are prepared we will know where to turn.

One lesson I have learned throughout my journey is that there will be tough times. There will be moments when I falter. Life will have its share of pains, problems, obstacles, and hardships. It is during these times when we will be weakest. The Devil will use these moments of weakness to tempt us to do things we normally wouldn't do. He will take the opportunity to make us question our beliefs, goals, and lives. He will definitely try to derail our efforts toward achieving God's plan for prosperity in our lives.

As is always the case, the best defense against these times will be a good offense. We will need to have tools at our disposal to help us remain strong in our faith. In my own life I have found a number of such tools. I use them when the times are good so that I will be prepared when something stands in the way of achieving the prosperous plans God has for me. The first disciples knew of these tools long before I did. Early on in the book of Acts we read: "They devoted themselves to the apostles' teaching and to the fellowship, to the breaking of bread and to prayer" (Acts 2:42). Let's get back to our roots. Let's follow the examples of the first followers of Christ and the early Church. To do this we must pray, read the Bible, fellowship with other believers, and go to church. Let's go through each of these four things individually.

PRAYER

"They devoted themselves to the apostles' teaching and to the fellowship, to the breaking of bread and to *prayer*."
—Acts 2:42

Prayer is the number one tool that God has given to prepare us for all things we will face in life. Prayer brings us closer to God and it helps us to understand what God wants of us. We can and should be praying all day long. Our entire lives should be a prayer to God. Each day should begin with a prayer and each night should end with one. We should never put a bite in our mouths without first acknowledging our God who gave it to us. We should always remember to confess our sins and to ask for forgiveness. We must give praise and honor to God through our prayers.

Many people think prayer is a last resort. I once had a friend in college that was dealing with some problems at the time. I asked him if he had prayed. His response was, "It hasn't come to that yet." I have run across many people in my life that share my friend's sentiment. These people call on God only when things are really bad.

A problem then becomes for these people that it's not always easy to reconnect with God. Our relationship with our creator is very similar to our human relationships. We can't go from not even acknowledging someone's existence to suddenly demanding that individual's attention. It takes time to develop the relationship. The more time we spend with a person the closer we will get to him. At some point the relationship will develop into one where you know you can rely on the other individual. Our relationship with God is the same. Through prayer we will develop our relationship with God over time. Then when obstacles start to surface, we will know and feel comfortable with turning to God.

God doesn't want to be a last resort. He wants to be in constant relationship with us. A primary tool in growing that relationship is through prayer. Prayer requires practice. The more we do it, the more second nature it will become. We will eventually find ourselves relying on prayer. The goal is to turn our lives over to God through it. Then we will know that no matter what problems may arise we can handle them through our prayers. Here is a closing thought on prayer: "Therefore let everyone who is godly pray to you while you may be found" (Psalm 32:6).

BIBLE

"They devoted themselves to the *apostles' teaching* and to the fellowship, to the breaking of bread and to prayer."
—Acts 2:42

Of course the early church didn't have a Bible to read. The Jews were familiar enough with the scrolls of the Old Testament but the early church wasn't all Jewish. Anyone who didn't personally know Jesus had to rely on eyewitness testimony and the teaching of the apostles. The apostles were taught directly by Jesus. It was their charge to spread the message of Christ to all those who would hear it. They did this through their preaching and teaching. Their preaching and teaching turned into letters to church communities and to the four gospels we have today.

The apostles' wisdom and understanding of the true living God, with whom they walked and talked, is contained in what is known today as the New Testament.

Is there any book more controversial than the Bible? I sure can't think of one. Merely mentioning the word *Bible* draws out the most polarized of emotions. Some people become disgusted and others are overjoyed. This wide array of emotion creates a stigma around reading the Bible. For someone not familiar with the text, reading the Bible can be a daunting task. People often don't even understand how or where they should start.

Many people that claim to be Christians haven't even opened a Bible in years. These same people will watch hours upon hours of TV each week without thinking to open the one book that promises to hold the key to their salvation and eternal happiness. One can't help but wonder how those individuals expect to realize God's plans in their lives if they don't even know what God wants to begin with. All that is left is to develop plans, and morals, and values based on our assumptions about God. But why assume when God gave us the blueprint for our lives in a book known as the Bible.

I know that I'm coming across harshly. It's all right though, because I'm talking about myself. It was only a couple years ago when I rarely, if ever, read the Bible. I claimed to be a follower of Christ and yet my only knowledge of Him came from other people. There have been a few times in my life when I have set out to read the Bible. I usually would start with Genesis only to get turned off by the time I reached Leviticus. I really struggled with the connection of the words that I was reading and my own life.

All of that changed a few years ago. Through prayer I decided to live a more Christ-like life. I then began reading various Christian books. These books put the Scriptures into context for me. I started to become obsessed and wanted to know more so I went to the source. I started to research things that I was curious about in the Bible. One of the first topics that I scoured the Bible for was prophecies. I was on a mission to find all of the Old Testament prophesies that were fulfilled in the New Testament and specifically in Jesus. This exercise led to other interests. At about this time I saw Mel Gibson's, *The Passion of the Christ*. It touched me so much that I wanted more. I decided to investigate the biblical accuracy of the movie so I decided to read all four gospel writers' accounts of Jesus' last days.

Like prayer, my experience with the Bible has been a slow process. It wasn't something that I just dove into. Little by little, though, I became used to reading the Bible. It is to the point now that one of my co-workers refers to me as a "Bible Junkie" to the students on the Encounter Retreats that we lead. I guess that I've become a little obsessed. I own and refer to several different versions of study Bibles. I know when circumstances arise that I'm not sure how to handle, I can turn to the Word of God for the answer. Here is a closing thought on the Bible: "Blessed is the one who reads the words of this prophecy, and blessed are those who hear it and take it to heart" (Revelation 1:3).

CHURCH

"They devoted themselves to the apostles' teaching and to the fellowship, to the **breaking of bread** and to prayer."

—Acts 2:42

I know Acts 2:24 doesn't say that the early followers went to church. Of course they didn't go to church. There was no church for the early Christians. It does say, however, that they were devoted to the *breaking of bread*. In this case it is indicative of the Lord's Supper as opposed to simply referring to sharing a meal. Verse 46 goes on to say: "Every day they continued to meet together in the temple courts." It is clear that the early believers felt the need to be near a holy place and to live a sacramental life.

Church is an often controversial subject on many different levels. There are so many questions that just mentioning the word *church* raises. Do you go to church or not? Do you believe in organized religion? What church do you go to? What denomination do you follow? Do you like the pastor? But church is not about any of those things. Church is about a community of people gathering together to give praise and glory to God. That's it, plain and simple. We are to raise our voices as one body to our Creator. Do you agree with that? If you said yes let me ask you another question. Why is it then that so many people are so concerned with what they get out of church? Church is supposed to be God-focused, not me-focused. Yet the number one reason believers state for not going to church (in my informal and unscientific study) is that they don't get anything out of it.

Now I know that it is true that different styles of worship appeal to different people. So find one that fits your style and go to it. It is important to note here that I'm not talking about denomination at all. I won't even touch on the subject. In 1 Samuel 16:7 God says to Samuel: "The Lord does not look at the things man looks at. Man looks at the outward appearance, but the Lord looks at the heart." Only God can judge the heart and therefore there is no point in arguing about denomination. What I am saying is to find the church you are comfortable with and go to it.

Remember, the main purpose of going to church is to give praise and glory to God in a community. Don't worry about what you get out of it at first. Concern yourself with the things that you give to it. Are your prayers, responses, and songs heartfelt and wholesome? Are you honestly giving praise and worship to God or are you waiting for the service or mass to be over. If you focus on giving to God during church I think you'll find that you'll get more out of it. The more you give, the more you'll get. It should get to a point that you really like and want to go to church. What excites you more—going to a movie on Friday night or going to church on Sunday morning? Think about that. You are going to be with God. Shouldn't that take priority over all other things? God will honor the time you spend with Him by blessing the time you spend elsewhere. Try it. Here is a closing thought on going to church: "Let us not give up meeting together, as some are in the habit of doing, but let us encourage one another" (Hebrews 10:25).

FELLOWSHIP

"They devoted themselves to the apostles' teaching and to the *fellowship*, to the breaking of bread and to prayer."
—Acts 2:42

Through our church community we can usually find a smaller group of believers with which to fellowship. Of course church isn't the only source of Christians that we can fellowship with. We are called to fellowship with all believers. There are many reasons why we should get together with other people that love the Lord. First, spending time with other believers brings pleasure to God. God loves when a group of people gather together and talk about Him. Think about all of the social gatherings in our lives. There are softball leagues and social clubs. We go to movies and sporting events. How many of them are Christ-centered? If someone were to make a judgment on our priorities based on what they see us doing what would he say? Fellowshipping with other believers is a way to show God that He is as important to us as these other worldly activities.

Fellowship also helps us to remember that we're not alone. There is so much in this world that does not bring glory to God. Listen to the radio. Watch your TV. Go to a movie. How many times must we shudder at what we see and hear? Anti-Christian values are reinforced continually throughout our world day in and day out. When we fellowship with other believers it helps us realize that we're not alone in our beliefs and values. We need this positive influence to combat all of the negative ones in the world around us. Without fellowship it would be so easy to go astray in this world. We would feel like it was OK because "everyone is doing it." Through fellowship we will see that contrary to common belief that *everyone* is not doing *it*, whatever *it* may be.

Fellowship gives us a support group to help us through the tough times. When difficult situations in our lives arise we will have people whom we can turn to for good advice. The advice and support they give us will not be worldly advice but instead, godly advice. Frequently when we are in these situations we may not think straight or won't be able to see a way out. By having a support group that we can trust, we can rely on their counsel to help get us back on our feet. Even if we are the type of people that don't like to rely on others we can still use their guidance to help calibrate our own emotions and decisions during that time. The key is to have this support group. They will be there for you and in turn you will be there for them.

In the school community where I work I also lead a faith-sharing group made up of members of the faculty. This group serves all of the above purposes; it gives glory to God; we realize that we are not alone in our problems and beliefs, and it has given us a support group that we can go to when we need them. I have found, though, that it also serves another purpose. Being a leader, I have to prepare my thoughts in an effort to direct the group. This extra reflection has helped me immensely with my own beliefs and faith. I recommend that if you are not already a part of such a group, you gather some believers and start one. Set out to do so in the next month and see where it goes.

Fellowship does not solely occur through organized small groups. Actually, it more frequently takes place through our day-to-day living. Identify yourself as a believer. Put a bumper sticker on your car. When someone talks about an amazing occurrence in their life tell them, "Thank God." Send an email to your friends of a spiritual nature. As you increasingly identify yourself as a Christian, opportunities to fellowship with other believers will present themselves.

I've been amazed with the results in my own life. It is really surprising how many people, who would give no indication otherwise, want to talk about God and their lives. They are just waiting to find another believer to share with or to ask advice from. So make an effort today to begin fellowshipping with other people about God. See what happens. Reflect on this

Scripture on fellowship as we close this thought: "For where two or three come together in my name, there I am with them" (Matthew 18:20).

PURGING

"If your right eye causes you to sin, gouge it out and throw it away. It is better for you to lose one part of your body than for your whole body to be thrown into hell. And if your right hand causes you to sin, cut it off and throw it away."

—Matthew 5:29, 30

I know that purging is not listed as part of that Acts verse. I'm not talking about throwing up here either. This is one tool that I added in myself. I think purging is a necessary tool for every Christian to use. Purging to me is getting rid of everything from one's life that is not pleasing to God. After all, why would God allow us to prosper if we would just use that prosperity to do and buy things that are offensive to Him? At first read this sounds like common sense.

Well, consider this. Imagine that you hear a knock on your front door. It's Jesus and He wants to have dinner with your family at your house. Would you be ashamed of the belongings that you and your family possess? Think hard. Do you have any magazines or books that you wouldn't want Jesus to know you read? Do you have DVDs you shouldn't watch? Are there posters on your children's walls that are not appropriate? Are there CDs in your collection that you shouldn't listen to? Are there photos in your albums that you wouldn't show Jesus? Are you, your spouse, or your children wearing clothing that is too explicit, revealing, or contains questionable printed content?

Are there websites in your "favorites" that you wouldn't want on the screen?

I'm not telling you how to feel or what's right or wrong. I'm just asking you some questions. If you answered yes to any of those questions then you should do one thing immediately. Quick, go and hide them (just kidding). Of course, Jesus already knows they are there, so don't go and hide everything now. Throw the items away. Burn them. Do whatever you think you should so that they are not a part of your life anymore. The reason for this will be twofold. First, you can then go to your Lord and Savior with a clear conscience about what you value in life. Second, you won't cause others to assume anything about you or go astray themselves because of what they perceive is OK in your life.

In my own life I found it hard to do this. I possessed all of those things mentioned above. I found it hard to part with them. I finally realized that if I'm to call myself a follower of Christ, then I don't want to possess anything in my life that I would not be proud to share with Him. When presented with that statement, it became easier to get rid of the things that needed to be purged.

Purging applies to activities also. For a while I tried to have it both ways. I wanted to be righteous in the eyes of God and others but I still did the things that I shouldn't do and went to places I shouldn't go. I told myself that I didn't have to sin but I could still be places where it was taking place. Boy, was I wrong. More times than not the temptation was too great and I reverted back to my old ways. I finally realized that in order to remain true to myself and my God, I would have to purge some activities and trips from my life. Here is a verse to think about: "Let us throw off everything that hinders and the sin that so easily entangles" (Hebrews 12:1).

GIVING

"Each man should give what he has decided in his heart to give, not reluctantly or under compulsion, for God loves a cheerful giver"

—2 Corinthians 9:7

Giving is also not listed in the Acts verse. I have included it in this chapter because I feel it is a crucial tool to our growth and ability to experience the prosperity that God has for us. God wants to know that we will share the gifts He gives us. In Chapter 5, we discussed prosperity and the Christian so we already know what happens to those that put money before God. We also know from that chapter that God will prosper those that love Him with all their hearts.

In my own life I have found that every time I have given of my money and time, I have gotten back even as much as ten times what I gave. Whenever I made a decision to give to a charity, church, or school, somehow money has found its way back into my hands. I'm serious. I've won awards, made money in the stock market, and received promotions. Each monetary gain was preceded by a decision and act of giving. One key thing to note here is that during none of those times was it the intention of my giving to gain in the end. It just happened that way and only recently have I realized it.

It is not my point to tell you how much to give or to whom to give it. I'm just telling you from my own experience that God will see in your life where your heart is. He wants to know where your trust is. Do you feel comfort in your life because you have prosperity or because you know that God has plans for you? He wants to be sure that if He gives you more that you will use it for His purposes. Consider the following: "Remember this: Whoever sows sparingly will also reap sparingly, and whoever sows generously will also reap generously" (2 Corinthians 9:6).

SUMMARY

We know from the Apostle Paul that we need to arm ourselves each and every day with tools that will prepare us for whatever we may encounter. These tools need to become a way of life. We must become accustomed to using them. This is not, after all, a concept unique to our spiritual walk. In many of our jobs, hobbies, interests and activities we have already applied the concepts of practicing, being prepared, and using tools as a precaution. It becomes so much more important to integrate these techniques into our quest to fulfill the prosperous plans that God has for us.

To develop an exhaustive list of everything that could help us achieve God's plan for our lives would take more pages than this book has. Through this chapter I have attempted to boil down all of the possible things that you can practice into a list of just six. The early followers of Christ also recognized this need for the routine application of tools in their own lives. The Bible says that these believers regularly prayed, fellowshipped, broke bread, and learned the apostles' teachings. In today's terms they prayed, fellowshipped, went to church, and read the Bible. From my own life experience I have found that those four things in conjunction with purging and giving will provide a solid foundation from which to grow one's faith and follow God's will.

It's a challenge, I know. But believe me it is necessary and becomes very fulfilling. So go ahead and give it a try. Pray. Fellowship. Go to church. Read the Bible. Purge. Give. Let me know how it turns out. I'd love to hear about it.

Chapter 14

LEARN HOW TO PLAY!—PUT IT ALL TOGETHER

"For I know the plans I have for you," declares the Lord, "plans to prosper you and not to harm you, plans to give you hope and a future. Then you will call upon me and come and pray to me, and I will listen to you. You will seek me and find me when you seek me with all your heart."

—Jeremiah 29:11-13

In the introduction to this book I made the following promise: "The purpose of this book is threefold. We will take a deep look inside of those words that inspire all who read them in an attempt to understand what exactly God means when He says, "For I know the plans I have for you." I will highlight the journey of my own life as a way to illustrate God's faithfulness to the promise that is Jeremiah 29. Last and most importantly, I will give practical steps and concrete actions that you can take to guarantee that you will fully realize the plans God has for your own life."

We've covered many concepts in this book that are related to Jeremiah 29:11-14. We took at look at the history of the verses and the words that comprise them. We've seen how just reading this Scripture offers people hope. I've recognized times in my own life and in the lives of those I know when doors have been miraculously opened. We know that God has great plans for us and we've studied what it means to love God with all our hearts. We know that our plans will at times be in conflict with God's plans and we've experienced times when God has given us signs of affirmation to let us know that we are on the right track. We are in agreement that in order to achieve the plans that Jeremiah 29 speaks about, we must act, and we have examined six tools we can use to help us to do just that.

Now that we've covered the aforementioned concepts and how they relate to Jeremiah 29, I will boil all of them down into four actionable steps that you can take to make Jeremiah 29 come alive in your own life. If you follow this plan you will grow closer to God. If you take this to heart you will live a fuller and happier life. You will begin to realize what God was talking about when He said: "For I know the plans I have for you," declares the Lord, "plans to prosper you and not to harm you, plans to give you hope and a future. Then you will call upon me and come and pray to me, and I will listen to you. You will seek me and find me when you seek me with all your heart" (Jeremiah 29:11-13).

There is an easy little acronym that I use to help remind me of the things that I must do to follow God's plan for me. I simply PLAY. If we PLAY we will be taking the necessary steps toward achieving God's will for our lives. When I think of the word PLAY, I think of children. In John 1, verses12 and 13, we read:

"Yet to all who received him, to those who believed in his name, he gave the right to become children of God—children born not of natural descent, nor of human decision or a husband's will, but born of God."

We all want to become a son or daughter of God. That is the goal. In Matthew 18, verses 3 and 4, Jesus says: "I tell you the truth, unless you change and become like little children, you will never enter the kingdom of heaven. Therefore, whoever humbles himself like this child is the greatest in the kingdom of heaven." Have you ever wondered what Jesus meant by these verses? Do you know why Jesus loved the little children so much? There are many reasons actually. Look at the qualities that children possess. Children are innocent, trusting, loving, and carefree. Children want attention from those they love and they give attention to those that love them. These are the qualities that make Jesus want to be with the children. It is for this reason that Jesus says: "Let the children come to me, and do not hinder them, for the kingdom of God belongs to such as these" (Luke 18:16).

So if we think of Jesus with the little children that He loved so much, we should have no trouble at all remembering the word PLAY. You're probably thinking to yourself, "All right already. What does PLAY stand for?" Well, I'll tell you. "P" is for PRAY. "L" stands for LISTEN. "A" begins the word ACT. "Y" represents the word YEARN. When you put it together you get PRAY, LISTEN, ACT, and YEARN. In these four steps you will begin to know what God wants for your life and how to attain those things.

Buried inside of the word PLAY are the three key steps to seeking and loving God with all of our hearts. From Chapter 11 we learned that the three steps are: listening to God, talking to God, and turning our lives over to God. Therefore, it should not be surprising that in order to follow God's plan for our lives we must do these three things. Remember, if Jeremiah 29, verse 11 is the promise, then verses 12 and 13 are the conditions of that promise. The condition, as we know, is to seek God with all of our hearts. So without further adieu, let's PLAY.

P IS FOR PRAY

Prayer is going to be one of your primary tools in helping you to fully realize God's plans for your life. Prayer is the key to seeking God with all our hearts. It is the way that we can connect with God on a daily basis. We can pray from almost anywhere. Some of my best and most intense prayers have occurred while kayaking down a river or during a climb up a mountain. Our life should be a praying life. If we don't talk to God how can we ever expect to know what He wants from us? If we don't develop this habit when things are OK how can we rely on it when they're not? Praying needs to become a way of life and not a last resort.

All right, so if you don't already pray, you need to start. Now! Go ahead and thank God for something in your life right now. Then get used to making it a part of your day. Pray in the morning when you wake up. Thank God for your day and ask Him for His guidance to get through it. Pray before meals. Pray while driving on the road. Get used to talking with God on a daily and even hourly basis. After a while, praying will just become natural to you. You will instinctively include God in your thoughts, conversations, and actions. Then when you really need God, you will feel Him close to you.

The goal is to develop a habit of prayer. But even if you haven't yet, you can still do this step of the word PLAY. You need to honestly present your needs to God. Tell Him your concerns. Ask for His help. Request His guidance. Don't worry. He already knows what you are going through. He really just wants to hear it from you. He wants you to acknowledge that you need Him. So do it. Do this whenever you don't know where to turn. Become accustomed to turning to God first. Offer up your worries to Him. I'm sure you'll be amazed at the results.

L IS FOR **LISTEN**

Once you have honestly and faithfully presented your needs to God, you need to listen. Remember, listening to God is the second step in learning to seek and love God with all of our hearts. Listen to what God is telling you. You'll feel it in your heart. That feeling you'll get is not just emotion. It's your inner self. God will be talking directly to you. He will connect with your heart. Try to make it go away if you want. Pray about it. See if it leaves you or just grows stronger.

Don't worry about the obstacles. Worry will only limit what your heart is telling you. Free yourself of worry. It's not healthy. Just sit and listen to your heart. Don't think about all the reasons your feeling won't work. You're dreaming, after all, and dreams are limitless. Let your imagination go. Feel God's presence in it. Where is it directing you? Once again, this is not the time to worry about why it won't work. Your job is to imagine how it could work.

God has given the human mind seemingly limitless potential. Long before humans were able to fly, people thought about soaring through the sky like a bird. Well in advance of computers, cellular phones, and digital cameras, people dreamed of the days they could talk to one another face-to-face across thousands of miles. What is your heart telling you to do? Use your mind to take what your heart is telling you and dream about it. Go back to step one and pray about it. Keep God in the loop. Ask Him if this feeling that He is giving you is really from Him. Listen to your heart. Listen to what God is telling you to do.

A IS FOR ACT

Without action life is meaningless. We've often heard that our actions speak louder than our words. Our actions will define what we become. Our actions will also let others know who is in control of our lives. Remember, the third part of loving God with all our hearts is to submit to His will and to turn our lives over to Him. Once we've prayed and listened, it then becomes time to act. If we don't act we can't fulfill the plans God has for us. We will never be able to prosper if we don't act.

Of course there is risk in taking action. It would be much easier to just keep things as they are. At least that's what we tell ourselves. Remember, if it is God's will it cannot fail. So there is actually more risk in not acting. I have a T-shirt with a message on the front that is continued on the back. The front reads: Are You Afraid to Die? The back follows it up with: Or Just Afraid to Live? I think that saying characterizes much of people's behavior today. We become so afraid of the risks that we end up missing out on life.

Actively follow up on whatever it was you prayed about and still feel led to do. If you prayed about it and you still feel like God is telling you to do it then you must begin to do it. Start researching what you need to do to make it happen. Strategize how you will fulfill the plan. Again, don't think of how the obstacles will stop you. Think about how you will overcome them and begin to do it. If you do not begin to work at God's plans you will never achieve them.

If you've prayed and listened, it is during the action that God will choose to direct you. Maybe your idea is not fully what God had in mind. That's OK. He will close the doors He wants closed and open the doors He wants opened. He will use your actions to lead you where He wants you to go. You want a road map. You got it. Begin to act and then follow where God leads you. He will take you step by step. The whole key is that you must ACT.

Y IS FOR YEARN

It is imperative throughout this process of praying, listening, and acting that we remain close to God. We need to yearn for God's love and guidance. Yearning for God will be accomplished by turning our lives completely over to God. Through this process we will need some tools to help keep us close to God. There will be struggles and we will need to be prepared. In the previous chapter I covered the six tools that I use regularly in my life to help keep me close to God. For easy reference I will list them here: Pray. Fellowship. Go to church. Read the Bible. Purge. Give. When I exercise each of these, I grow closer to God. I want to be with God. I yearn for God.

Yearning for God will carry us through the tough times. It will help to keep us focused. We will remember what is important. We will be seeking God with all our hearts. If we seek God with all our hearts we will find God. When we find God He will bring us back from our captivity. He will allow us to fully realize the plans of prosperity that He has for us. He wants to see and feel us yearn for Him.

There is another important factor at play with yearning. When we yearn for God, others will notice. This is one of our main callings in life. Second to loving God with all our hearts is showing God's love to our neighbors. We must be a witness of Jesus Christ to those around us. Through our yearning for God we will want to share our joy with others. They will see it in us. Therefore, in yearning for God we will not only grow closer ourselves but those around us will also grow to know God. God will honor that in our lives.

SUMMARY

So I ask you now to think. Think about your life. Are you feeling as though you should be doing something else? Do you feel there are things you should start or stop doing? Are you living out Jeremiah 29 in your life? Do you seek God with all your heart? What do you feel deep down inside? Are you fulfilling God's plans for you?

Only you know the answers to the questions. No one can tell you what you are supposed to do, no one that is, except for God. Are you willing to pursue God's mission for your life? If the answer is yes then I urge you to take to heart the lessons in this book. Begin your journey today. Go ahead and start to PLAY now. *Pray* to God about your life and acknowledge His sovereignty over it. Thank Him for what He has given you and ask for His guidance in achieving His will. Then *Listen* to what He has to tell you. Feel where He is directing you. Dream about what He wants you to do. Once you've prayed and listened, it becomes time to *Act*. Don't wait a moment longer than you need to. Put away your reservations and worries and know that because it is God's will you cannot fail. And through this whole process continue to *Yearn* for God. Continue to grow in Him. Revisit each of the steps as necessary.

On a final note, we must remember that the path God has for each of our lives is different. We must do our own part in achieving the goals God has for us. This may take much time and sacrifice. It will include obstacles and struggles. Our success is not defined in comparison to others but instead we must look deep within our hearts in order to receive the prize. Then and only then will we realize the fullness of the prosperity God has for us. That prosperity is the peace of knowing we have followed God's lead in our lives and that we may be rewarded for it in this life, and we definitely will be rewarded for it in the next. Only God's time will tell, as it is written in Galatians 6:9: "Let us not become weary in doing good, for at the proper time we will reap a harvest if we do not give up."

Let us close this chapter and book with a prayer. I invite you to say your own prayer. Say a prayer that comes from your heart. If you aren't used to that yet, then I have included here a similar prayer to the one at the end of Chapter 3. If you choose to use this prayer concentrate on truly feeling and meaning the words. Pray it with all your heart.

Dear Lord,

You are so wonderful in all You are and in all You do. Thank You for choosing to know me. Thank You for loving me. I know the promise that You have given us in Jeremiah 29 and I believe in the power of this promise. I believe You have plans that involve good things for me. I believe that

You don't want me to live just a mediocre life. You want me to live a life with prosperity. Please help me to do the things necessary in order for Your plans to be fulfilled. Open the doors You want opened and close the doors You want closed. And Lord, give me the strength and courage to go through the doors You will miraculously open. Give me the strength to follow You and to seek You with all my heart. Help me to be like the little children so that I, too, may inherit the kingdom of God....(go ahead and add your words here), *I ask this in Jesus' name. Amen.*

A LETTER FROM THE AUTHOR

*"Trust in the Lord and do good; dwell in the land and enjoy safe pasture. **Delight yourself in the Lord and he will give you the desires of your heart.** Commit your way to the Lord; trust in him and he will do this: He will make your righteousness shine like the dawn, the justice of your cause like the noonday sun."*
—Psalm 37:3-6

Dear Readers:

Thank you for allowing me to take this journey with you. I am confident that if you take to heart the lessons in this book and do the steps I have outlined in the last four chapters, you will fully realize the plans God has to prosper you. You will achieve them in this life and more importantly you will enjoy His plans for you in the next. You will know and understand the words in Jeremiah 29:11-13.

If you enjoyed this book I encourage you to contact me and let me know your thoughts. You can reach me through my website at **www.plans2prosperU.com.** I would also like to invite you to sign up to receive my free monthly electronic newsletter. In it you'll find inspirational Scripture passages, thoughts for the month, and stories relating to the topics of this book, as well as some great deals on some of my other products. Please feel free to tell your friends about this book, my website, and the free monthly newsletter.

I also have plans for a journal to go along with this book. It should be available shortly. In it you will find guided exercises to applying these concepts in your own life. It can be used as a companion to this book or as a stand-alone guide. I encourage you to go to my website for more details on how to obtain the *Plans to Prosper You Life Journal.*

This writing has been a long journey for me and many thoughts have raced through my head along the way. While typing the very words you are reading, I found myself asking many of the same questions included in these pages. Through it all God has directed my work. I can only hope and pray that I have accurately transcribed the text that He has authored. It is my ultimate goal in this writing that you will grow closer to our Lord and Savior, Jesus Christ, through it. I'd like to end this letter the way that this project began, with a message from God:

"For I know the plans I have for you," declares the Lord, "plans to prosper you and not to harm you, plans

to give you hope and a future. Then you will call upon me and come and pray to me, and I will listen to you. You will seek me and find me when you seek me with all your heart" (Jeremiah 29:11-13 NIV).
God Bless,

George E. Sayour

P.S. Don't forget to check out my website: www.plans2prosperU.com.

Appendixes

"For I know the plans I have for you," declares the Lord, "plans to prosper you and not to harm you, plans to give you hope and a future. Then you will call upon me and come and pray to me, and I will listen to you. You will seek me and find me when you seek me with all your heart. I will be found by you," declares the Lord, "and will bring you back from captivity. I will gather you from all the nations and places where I have banished you," declares the Lord, "and bring you back to the place from which I carried you into exile."

—Jeremiah 29:11-14

APPENDIX A: NOTES

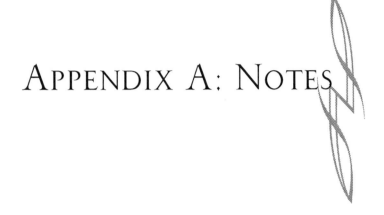

I. The Significance and Implications of Jeremiah 29
   A. Jeremiah 29 in Today's World
      1) All who read Jeremiah 29 find hope in its words.
      2) God will open and close doors to help us achieve His plans.
      3) The prosperity that Jeremiah 29 speaks about is one of a fullness of peace.
   B. Lessons from the History of Jeremiah 29
      1) For every action there is an equal and opposite reaction.
      2) Even though we fall, God wants to bring us back to Him.
      3) God wants us to prosper now in our current situation as well as in the future.
      4) God's promises apply to us as much as when they were originally spoken.

C. Wrong Turns on the Way to Achieving God's Plans for Us
  1) The Path of Least Resistance
  2) The Fast Lane
  3) The Scenic Route
  4) The Road of Regrets, Depression, Worry, and Anxiety

D. Prosperity and the Christian
  1) The OT describes a cause and effect relationship for achieving prosperity.
  2) The NT warns of the traps of putting money before God.
  3) God will use people of wealth and power to carry out His plans.

E. The Specific Words of Jeremiah 29:11-14
  1) Verse 11 is the promise.
  2) Verses 12 and 13 are the conditions of the promise.
  3) The key is to seek God with all our hearts.

II. God's Use of Jeremiah 29 in Our Lives
  A. Signs of Affirmation
    1) God will open and close the necessary doors.
    2) God will put people in your path right when you need them.
    3) God will give you obvious rewards to let you know.

  B. God's Work in Our Lives
    1) God will allow discontent to seep into our lives as we grow away from Him.
    2) God will use the discontent in our lives to bring us back to Him.

206

3) Sometimes things will get worse before they get better, even after a change.
4) God's plans will always be better than our own.
5) God will give us signs of affirmation to direct us and to show His pleasure.
6) God's plans for us are a continual process that never ends.

B. The Author's Story
1) Growing up: Florida
   - Safe Environment
   - Lots of Family
   - Christian Household
2) Private Religious Schools Grades K through 12
   - Ran cross-country and track
   - Graduated with honors
   - Attended Encounter Retreat
3) Rensselaer Polytechnic Institute: New York.
   - BS mechanical engineering
   - Minor in management
   - Co-op job with Southco, Inc
4) Procter & Gamble: Pennsylvania
   - Money
   - Responsibility
   - Travel
   - Discontent
   - Grow apart from self, others, and God
5) Time for a Change: Florida
   - Seek to follow God's will in life
   - Math teacher

- Cross-country coach
- Encounter Retreat leader
- Teacher of the Year
- Director of Admissions
- Grow closer to self, others, and God
- Marry Susan
- Strive to live out Jeremiah 29 on a daily basis

III. Practical Steps in Applying Jeremiah 29 to Your Own Life

  A. Love God with All Your Heart

    1) Listen to God.

    2) Talk to God.

    3) Turn your life over to God.

  B. Put on the Full Armor of God

    1) Pray to God.

    2) Go to church.

    3) Read the Bible.

    4) Fellowship with other believers.

    5) Purge from your life anything that is not pleasing to God.

    6) Give of yourself, your time, and your money.

  C. Learn to PLAY: Getting Started

    1) Pray about your current concern.

    2) Listen to what God is telling you.

    3) Act on the message that God gives you.

    4) Yearn to grow closer to God through the process.

APPENDIX B: CHAPTER BY CHAPTER SCRIPTURE USAGE

The New International Version (NIV) of the Bible has been my primary source for most of my Scripture usage. The NIV takes into account the literal meaning of the original texts as well as the historical context in which they were written. The New International Version is the most widely sold English translation of the Bible and therefore it is likely that many of you also own this version.

That, however, is not an indication that I feel the NIV is superior to the other translations that are available. I currently own the following different versions of the Bible: KJV, NKJV, NIV, NCV, NAB, NLT, TEV, The Geneva Bible, The Message, and even The Picture Bible from my childhood. It is my belief that whenever studying a Scripture one should do so from many different angles as we did in Chapter 4.

On another note, you may have noticed that in some cases I used only a short phrase out of a whole verse of Scripture. It has been my experience that when asking God specific questions that He will direct my study in this manner. He will focus my eyes onto a certain part of a verse and speak to me through it. Therefore, I have quoted these Scriptures as the parts that pertain to our study.

On the following pages I have included all of the Scripture passages used throughout this book. They are arranged by chapter and with little to no supporting material. Many of these Scripture passages are among my favorites and as such I wanted to offer them to all of you in an easily accessible manner. This way if you remember that you liked a certain verse but don't remember the specific page it was on you can simply look chapter by chapter through this appendix.

FOREWORD

"For I know the plans I have for you," declares the Lord, "plans to prosper you and not to harm you, plans to give you hope and a future. Then you will call upon me and come and pray to me, and I will listen to you. You will seek me and find me when you seek me with all your heart I will be found by you," declares the Lord, "and will bring you back from captivity. I will gather you from all the nations and places where I have banished you," declares the Lord, "and bring you back to the place from which I carried you into exile."

—Jeremiah 29:11-14

"But remember the Lord your God, for it is he who gives you the ability to produce wealth, and so confirms His covenant, which He swore to your forefathers, as it is today."

—Deuteronomy 8:18

"I pray that you may prosper in all things and be in health just as your soul prospers"

—3 John 1:2 NKJV

"I have come that they may have life, and have it to the full."

—John 10:10

CHAPTER 1: DOORS WILL BE OPENED

"Ask and it will be given to you; seek and you will find; knock and the door will be opened to you. For everyone who asks receives; he who seeks finds; and to him who knocks the door will be opened."

—Matthew 7:7, 8

"For I know the plans I have for you," declares the Lord, "plans to prosper you and not to harm you, plans to give you hope and a future. Then you will call upon me and come and pray to me, and I will listen to you. You will seek me and find me when you seek me with all your heart."

—Jeremiah 29:11-13

"Come to me, all you who are weary and burdened, and I will give you rest."

—Matthew 11:28

"Whether you turn to the right or to the left, your ears will hear a voice behind you, saying, 'This is the way; walk in it.'"

—Isaiah 30:21

CHAPTER 2: THE HISTORY BEHIND JEREMIAH 29

"Thus says the Lord of Hosts, the God of Israel, to all who were carried away captive, whom I have caused to be carried away from Jerusalem to Babylon…"

—Jeremiah 29:4 NKJV

"If you walk in My statutes and keep My commandments, and perform them, then…"

—Leviticus 26:3

"But if you do not obey Me, and do not observe all these commandments…"

—Leviticus 26:3

"Build houses and settle down; plant gardens and eat what they produce. Marry and have sons and daughters in marriage, so that they too may have sons and daughters. Increase in number there; do not decrease. Also, seek the peace and prosperity of the city to which I have carried you into exile. Pray to the Lord for it, because if it prospers, you too will prosper."

—Jeremiah 29:5-7

"'Do not let the prophets and diviners among you deceive you. Do not listen to the dreams you encourage them to have. They are prophesying lies to you in my name. I have not sent them' declares the Lord."

—Jeremiah 29:8, 9

"When seventy years are completed for Babylon, I will come to you and fulfill my gracious promise to bring you back to this place."

—Jeremiah 29:10

"For I know the plans I have for you," declares the Lord, "plans to prosper you and not to harm you, plans to give you hope and a future. Then you will call upon me and come and pray to me, and I will listen to you. You will seek me and find me when you seek me with all your heart."

—Jeremiah 29:11-13

"I will be found by you," declares the Lord, "and will bring you back from captivity. I will gather you from all the nations and places where I have banished you," declares the Lord, "and bring you back to the place from which I carried you into exile."

—Jeremiah 29:14

"...I, Daniel, understood by the books the number of years specified by the word of the Lord through Jeremiah the prophet, that He would accomplish seventy years in the desolation of Jerusalem."

—Daniel 9:2 NKJV

"It is I who says of Cyrus, 'He is My shepherd, and he shall perform all My pleasure, saying to Jerusalem, 'You shall be built,' and to the temple, 'Your foundation shall be laid'"

—Isaiah 44:28

"Now in the first year of Cyrus king of Persia, that the word of the Lord by the mouth of Jeremiah might be fulfilled, the Lord stirred up the spirit of Cyrus the king of Persia, so that he made a proclamation throughout all his kingdom"

—Ezra 1:1

CHAPTER 3: THE JOURNEY OF LIFE

"Enter through the narrow gate. For wide is the gate and broad is the road that leads to destruction, and many enter through it. But small is the gate and narrow the road that leads to life, and only a few find it."

—Matthew 7:13, 14

PATH OF LEAST RESISTANCE

"Whatever you do, work at it with all your heart, as working for the Lord, not for men."

—Colossians 3:23

THE FAST LANE

"…Mary, who sat at the Lord's feet listening to what he said. But Martha was distracted by all the preparations that had to be made. She came to him and asked, 'Lord, don't you care that my sister has left me to do the work by myself?'"

—Luke 10:39, 40

"…you are worried and upset about many things, but only one thing is needed. Mary has chosen what is better, and it will not be taken away from her"

—Luke 10:41, 42

THE SCENIC ROUTE

"But one thing I do: Forgetting what is behind and straining toward what is ahead, I press on toward the goal to win the prize for which God has called me heavenward in Christ Jesus."

—Philippians 3:13, 14

The Road of Regrets, Worry, Depression, and Anxiety

"Therefore I tell you, do not worry about your life, what you will eat; or about your body, what you will wear. Life is more than food, and the body more than clothes. Consider the ravens: They do not sow or reap, they have no storeroom or barn; yet God feeds them. And how much more valuable you are than birds! Who of you by worrying can add a single hour to his life?"

—Luke 12:22-25

The Call

"Rejoice in the Lord always. Again I will say, rejoice!"

—Philippians 4:4 NKJV

Chapter 4: A Study of the Words of Jeremiah 29:11-13

"The unfolding of your words gives light."

—Psalm 119:130

"Then you call on the name of your gods, and I will call on the name of the Lord; and the god who answers by fire, He is God."

—1 Kings 18:24 NKJV

"But from there you will seek the Lord your God, and you will find Him, if you seek Him with all of your heart and with all of your soul. When you are in distress and these things come upon you in the latter days, when you turn to the Lord your God and obey His voice (for the Lord your God is a merciful

God), He will not forsake you nor destroy you, nor forget the covenant of your fathers which He swore to them"

—Deuteronomy 4:29, 30 NKJV

THE PROMISE

"For I know the thoughts that I think toward you," saith the Lord, "thoughts of peace, and not of evil, to give you an expected end"

—Jeremiah 29:11 KJV

"For I know the plans I have for you," declares the Lord, "plans to prosper you and not to harm you, plans to give you hope and a future."

—Jeremiah 29:11 NIV

"For surely I know the plans I have for you," says the Lord, "plans for your welfare and not for harm, to give you a future with hope."

—Jeremiah 29:11 NSRV

"I say this because I know what I am planning for you," says the Lord, " I have good plans for you, not plans to hurt you. I will give you hope and a good future."

—Jeremiah 29:11 NCV

"For I know the thoughts that I think toward you," says the Lord, "thoughts of peace and not of evil, to give you a future and a hope."

—Jeremiah 29:11 NKJV

THE CONDITION

"Then shall ye call upon me, and ye shall go and pray unto me, and I will hearken unto you. And ye shall seek me, and find me, when ye shall search for me with all you heart."

—Jeremiah 29:12, 13 KJV

"Then you will call upon me and come and pray to me, and I will listen to you. You will seek me and find me when you seek me with all your heart."

—Jeremiah 29:12, 13 NIV

"Then when you call upon me and come and pray to me, I will hear you. When you search for me, you will find me; if you seek me with all your heart."

—Jeremiah 29:12, 13 NSRV

"Then you will call my name. You will come to me and pray to me and I will listen to you. You will search for me. And when you search for me with all your heart, you will find Me!"

—Jeremiah 29:12, 13 NCV

"Then you will call upon Me and go and pray to Me, and I will listen to you. And you will seek Me and find Me, when you search for Me with all your heart."

—Jeremiah 29:12, 13 NKJV

CHAPTER 5: PROSPERITY AND THE CHRISTIAN

"What good will it be for a man if he gains the whole world, yet he forfeits his soul."

—Matthew 16:26

"I have come that they may have life, and have it to the full"

—John 10:10

"Carefully follow the terms of this covenant, so that you may prosper in everything you do."

—Deuteronomy 29:9

"I am making this covenant, with its oath, not only with you who are standing here with us today in the presence of the Lord our God but also with those who are not here today."

—Deuteronomy 29:14

"Love the Lord your God with all your heart and with all you soul and with all your mind and with all your strength. The second is this: Love your neighbor as yourself."

—Matthew 22:37-3

"All the Law and the Prophets hang on these two commandments."

—Matthew 22:40

"Then the Lord your God will restore your fortunes."

—Deuteronomy 30:2

"The Lord will grant you abundant prosperity…"

—Deuteronomy 28:11

"…but he who trusts in the Lord will prosper."

—Proverbs 28:25

"Wealth and honor come from you."

—1 Chronicles 29:12

"…when God gives any man wealth and possessions…"

—Ecclesiastes 5:19

JABEZ

"Jabez cried out to the God of Israel, 'Oh that you would bless me and enlarge my territory! Let your hand be with me, and keep me from harm so that I will be free from pain.' And God granted his request."

—I Chronicles 4:10

KING DAVID

"The Lord does not look at the things that man looks at. Man looks at outward appearance, but the Lord looks at the heart."

—1 Samuel 16:7

"The Lord has sought out a man after his own heart and appointed him leader of his people."

—1 Samuel 13:14

"He died at a good old age, having enjoyed long life, wealth, and honor."

—1 Chronicles 29:28

"Walk in His ways, and keep His decrees and commands, His laws and requirements, as written in the Law of Moses, that you may prosper in all you do and wherever you go."

—1 Kings 2:3

KING SOLOMON

"Solomon showed his love for the Lord by walking according to the statutes of his father David."

—1 Kings 3:3

"So give your servant a discerning heart to govern your people and to distinguish between right and wrong."

—1 Kings 3:9

"Moreover, I will give you what you have not asked for—both riches and honor."

—1 Kings 3:13

"King Solomon was greater in riches and wisdom than all the other kings of the earth."

—2 Chronicles 9:22

RUTH

"Don't urge me to leave you or to turn back from you. Where you go I will go, and where you stay I will stay. Your people will be my people and your God my God."

—Ruth 1:6

BOAZ

"…a man of great wealth."

—Ruth 2:1 NKJV

"Just then, Boaz arrived from Bethlehem and greeted the harvesters, 'The Lord be with you!'"

—Ruth 2:4 NKJV

ABRAM

"Abram had become very wealthy in livestock and in silver
and gold."

—Genesis 13:2

ISAAC

"The man became rich, and his wealth continued…"

—Genesis 26:13

JOSEPH

"The Lord was with Joseph and he prospered"

—Genesis 39:2

BARZILLAI

"…for he was a very wealthy man"

—2 Samuel 19:32

JEHOSHAPHAT

"He had great wealth and honor, his heart was devoted to
the ways of the Lord."

—2 Chronicles 17:5,6

HEZEKIAH

"…for God had given him very great riches."

—2 Chronicles 32:29

JOB

"The Lord made him prosperous again, and gave him twice
as much as he had."

—Job 4:10

NEW TESTAMENT

"For the love of money is a root of all kinds of evil."
—1 Timothy 6:10

"What must I do to inherit eternal life?"
—Mark 10:17

"Children, how hard it is to enter the kingdom of God! It is easier for a camel to go through the eye of a needle than for a rich man to enter the kingdom of God."
—Mark 10:24-25

"Who then can be saved?"
—Mark 10:26

"With man this is impossible, but not with God; all things are possible with God."
—Mark 10:27

"I have not come to abolish them but to fulfill them."
—Matthew 5:17

"But seek first his kingdom and his righteousness, and all these things will be given to you as well."
—Matthew 6:33

"Zacchaeus was a chief tax collector and was wealthy."
—Luke 19:2

"Today salvation has come to this house."
—Luke 19:9

"I pray that you may prosper in all things and be in health just as your soul prospers."

—3 John 1:2 NKJV

People of Prosperity Who Are Used for God's Will

"You shall be in charge of my palace, and all my people are to submit to your orders. Only with respect to the throne will I be greater than you"

—Genesis 41:40

"As evening approached, there came a rich man from Arimathea, named Joseph, who had himself become a disciple of Jesus."

—Matthew 27:57

"Command those who are rich in this present world not to be arrogant nor to put their hope in wealth, which is so uncertain, but to put their hope in God, who richly provides us with everything for our enjoyment. Command them to do good, to be rich in good deeds, and to be generous and willing to share. In this way they will lay up treasure for themselves as a firm foundation for the coming age, so that they may take hold of the life that is truly life."

—1 Timothy 6:17

Chapter 6: Be Careful What You Wish for—Achieving Success

"Delight yourself in the Lord and he will give you the desires of your heart"

—Psalm 37:4

"Love the Lord your God with all your heart and with all your soul and with all your mind. This is the first and greatest commandment. And the second is like it: Love your neighbor as yourself. All the Law and the Prophets hang on these two commandment."

—Matthew 37-40

"What good will it be for a man if he gains the whole world, yet he forfeits his soul."

—Matthew 16:26

CHAPTER 7: WORSE BEFORE BETTER

"When you pass through the waters, I will be with you; and when you pass through the rivers they will not sweep over you. When you walk through the fire, you will not be burned; the flames will not set you ablaze."

—Isaiah 43:2

"...all the days ordained for me were written in your book before one of them came to be."

—Psalm 139:16

CHAPTER 8: OUR PLANS VS. GOD'S PLANS

"No eye has seen, no ear has heard, no mind has conceived what God has prepared for those who love him."

—1 Corinthians 2:9

"For I know the plans I have for you," declares the Lord, "plans to prosper you and not to harm you, plans to give you hope and a future. Then you will call upon me and come and pray to me, and I will listen to you. You will seek me and find me when you seek me with all your heart."

—Jeremiah 29:11-13

CHAPTER 9: ATTA BOY!—SIGNS OF AFFIRMATION

"Therefore the Lord himself will give you a sign."

—Isaiah 7:14

"Call to me and I will answer you and tell you great and unsearchable things you do not know. For this is what the Lord, God of Israel, says."

—Jeremiah 33:3

"Nevertheless, I will bring health and healing to it; I will heal my people and will let them enjoy abundant peace and security."

—Jeremiah 33:6

"I will cleanse them from all the sin they have committed against me and will forgive all their sins of rebellion against me. Then this city will bring me renown, joy, praise and honor before all nations on earth that hear of all the good things I do for it; and they will be in awe and tremble at the abundant prosperity and peace I provide for it."

—Jeremiah 33:8

CHAPTER 10: GOD ISN'T FINISHED WITH ME YET—GOD'S TIMING

"Being confident of this, that he who began a good work in you will carry it on to completion until the day of Christ Jesus."

—Philippians 1:6

"Jesus loved Martha and her sister and Lazarus. Lazarus became sick while Jesus was away. Yet when he heard Lazarus was sick, he stayed where he was two more days."

—John 11:5-6

"This sickness will not end in death. No, it is for God's glory so that God's Son may be glorified."

—John 11:4

"I am the resurrection and the life. He who believes in me will live, even though he dies; and whoever lives and believes in me will never die. Do you believe this?"

—John 11:25, 26

"Do not be afraid, Daniel. Since the first day that you set your mind to gain understanding and to humble yourself before God, your words were heard, and I have come in response to them."

—Daniel 10:12

"But I know that even now God will give you whatever you ask"

—John 11:22

226

CHAPTER 11: IT'S A MATTER OF THE HEART

"You will seek me and find me when you seek me with all
your heart."

—Jeremiah 29:13

"Love the Lord your God with all your heart and with all
your soul and with all your mind."

—Matthew 22:37

"What shall we do with the ark of the Lord? Tell us how we
should send it back to its place."

—1 Samuel 6:2

"Do not conform any longer to the pattern of this world, but
be transformed by the renewing of your mind. Then you will
be able to test and approve what God's will is—His good,
pleasing, and perfect will."

—Romans 12:2

"Therefore I tell you, do not worry about your life, what
you will eat; or about your body, what you will wear. Life is
more than food, and the body more than clothes. Consider
the ravens: They do not sow or reap, they have no storeroom
or barn; yet God feeds them. And how much more valuable
you are than birds!"

—Luke 12:22-24

CHAPTER 12: GO FOR IT!—TAKING RISKS

"I can do all things through Christ who strengthens me."

—Philippians 4:13 NKJV

"If God is for us, who can be against us?"

—Romans 8:31

"For I know the plans I have for you," declares the Lord, "plans to prosper you and not to harm you."

—Jeremiah 29:11

CHAPTER 13: PROTECT YOURSELF— USING THE RIGHT TOOLS

"Therefore put on the full armor of God, so that when the day of evil comes, you may be able to stand your ground."

—Ephesians 6:13

"Therefore put on the full armor of God, so that when the day of evil comes, you may be able to stand your ground, and after you have done everything, to stand. Stand firm then, with the belt of truth buckled around your waist, with the breastplate of righteousness in place, and with your feet fitted in readiness that comes from the gospel of peace. In addition to all this, take up the shield of faith, with which you can extinguish all the flaming arrows of the evil one. Take the helmet of salvation and the sword of the Spirit, which is the word of God. And pray in the Spirit on all occasions."

—Ephesians 6:13-18

"They devoted themselves to the apostles' teaching and to the fellowship, to the breaking of bread and to prayer."

—Acts 2:42

PRAY TO GOD

"Therefore let everyone who is godly pray to you while you may be found."

—Psalm 32:6

228

READ THE BIBLE

"Blessed is the one who reads the words of this prophecy, and blessed are those who hear it and take it to heart."

—Revelation 1:3

GO TO CHURCH

"Every day they continued to meet together in the temple courts."

—Acts 2:42

"The Lord does not look at the things man looks at. Man looks at the outward appearance, but the Lord looks at the heart."

—1 Samuel 16:7

"Let us not give up meeting together, as some are in the habit of doing, but let us encourage one another."

—Hebrews 10:25

FELLOWSHIP WITH OTHER BELIEVERS

"For where two or three come together in my name, there I am with them."

—Matthew 18:20

PURGE UNGODLINESS FROM YOUR LIFE

"If your right eye causes you to sin, gouge it out and throw it away. It is better for you to lose one part of your body than for your whole body to be thrown into hell. And if your right hand causes you to sin, cut it off and throw it away"

—Matthew 5:29, 30

"Let us throw off everything that hinders and the sin that so easily entangles."

—Hebrews 12:1

GIVE OF YOUR MONEY AND TIME

"Each man should give what he has decided in his heart to give, not reluctantly or under compulsion, for God loves a cheerful giver"

—2 Corinthians 9:7

"Remember this: Whoever sows sparingly will also reap sparingly, and whoever sows generously will also reap generously"

—2 Corinthians 9:6

CHAPTER 14: LEARN HOW TO PLAY— PUT IT ALL TOGETHER

"For I know the plans I have for you," declares the Lord, "plans to prosper you and not to harm you, plans to give you hope and a future. Then you will call upon me and come and pray to me, and I will listen to you. You will seek me and find me when you seek me with all your heart."

—Jeremiah 29:11-13

"Yet to all who received him, to those who believed in his name, he gave the right to become children of God—children born not of natural descent, nor of human decision or a husband's will, but born of God."

—John 1:12-13

"I tell you the truth, unless you change and become like little children, you will never enter the kingdom of heaven.

Therefore, whoever humbles himself like this child is the greatest in the kingdom of heaven."

—Matthew 18:3, 4

"Let the children come to me, and do not hinder them, for the kingdom of God belongs to such as these."

—Luke 18:16

"Let us not become weary in doing good, for at the proper time we will reap a harvest if we do not give up."

—Galatians 6:9

A LETTER FROM THE AUTHOR

"Trust in the Lord and do good: dwell in the land and enjoy safe pasture. Delight yourself in the Lord and he will give you the desires of your heart. Commit your way to the Lord; trust in him and he will do this: He will make your righteousness shine like the dawn, the justice of your cause like the noonday sun."

—Psalm 37:3-6

APPENDIX C:
LETTERS FROM HOME

Included here are three letters I received while on the Encounter Retreat that I participated in when I was a junior in high school. In each of these letters are words of deep wisdom. These words have been at the root of my upbringing and still ring true today. I am so thankful to God for giving me my parents and grandparents that have become my mentors and friends.

January 29, 1992

Dear George,

As your grandparents we are commissioned by God to be concerned with all aspects of your life. This is especially true about your walk with Jesus! We want Him to be the Lord of your life. **It will only happen as you open up your heart to Him and allow Him to do what He wants to do in you!** We know that God will be more real to you as He reveals Himself and you receive what He has for you...

We love you very much,

Grandma and Grandpa

January 29, 1992

Dear George,

I believe this Encounter that you are undertaking, if taken seriously, and God willing it will be, will prove to be the most important thing in all of your life. If done properly, with an open mind and an **open heart**, you will have an open soul. **You will be able to find God like never before; you will be able to know the Lord Jesus** like you have never known Him before and you will find yourself perhaps like never before. In the lectures, in your prayers and in your meditations the one key word here is to "LISTEN." Listen carefully to the Lord and you will hear Him. He will open up your heart and soul so that you will not only hear Him but you will be able to FEEL HIM within you. His Holy Spirit will live within you and you will feel His love for you. You will learn to love the Lord your God and Maker like you have never loved Him before. Again, LISTEN and you will HEAR, you will LEARN, and you will LOVE. All of that is there for the asking. Ask Him into your life and HE will be there for you always. I pray that He will be your best friend as He is mine. When in trouble always invoke His name and never forget to give thanks and glory to God in all things. **Always remember that all that we are comes from God. All that we have comes from God.** All of our dependence is on God. We must have Faith in God that He will be there for us, that He will never desert us and that **He will care for our needs as He sees fit. We must always depend on Him, for all comes from Him...** George, I love you dearly and I ask God to bless you now and always that you will be enriched for the rest of your life.

> Love always,
> Dad

January 29, 1992

Dear George,

This Encounter that you are embarking on is another step in life's journey. If you do not have a personal relationship with the Lord, life is meaningless. **Remember that in making decisions to always pray and ask the Lord for guidance and wisdom. He will guide you in all that you do if you follow His will.** He is faithful. He is our hope and you need to put your trust in Him to see you through the good and bad times. God has something special in mind for you. **Seek His will in all you do.** Also, don't forget that He wants you to have fun, too.

Always remember that we are so blessed to have the family that we do. Life is full of memories, "pictures in our mind." Making memories is a daily routine. Friends, family, traditions will be in our memories always. Our family is special and we have to help each other to stick together. Don't forget that people and relationships are what are important. Let God show you the way...

I love you,

Mom

Printed in the United States
79921LV00001B/1-123